Instructor's Resource Manual for
Samovar and Porter's

Intercultural Communication
A Reader

Eighth Edition

Lisa A. Stefani
San Diego State University

Lisa M. Skow
Indiana State University

Larry A. Samovar
San Diego State University

Wadsworth Publishing Company
I(T)P® An International Thomson Publishing Company

Belmont • Albany • Bonn • Boston • Cincinnati • Detroit • London • Madrid • Melbourne
Mexico City • New York • Paris • San Francisco • Singapore • Tokyo • Toronto • Washington

Wadsworth Publishing Company
10 Davis Drive
Belmont, California 94002, USA

International Thomson Publishing Europe
Berkshire House 168-173
High Holborn
London, WC1V 7AA, England

Thomas Nelson Australia
102 Dodds Street
South Melbourne 3205
Victoria, Australia

Nelson Canada
1120 Birchmount Road
Scarborough, Ontario
Canada M1K 5G4

International Thomson Editores
Campos Eliseos 385, Piso 7
Col. Polanco
11560 México D.F. México

International Thomson Publishing GmbH
Königswinterer Strasse 418
53227 Bonn, Germany

International Thomson Publishing Asia
221 Henderson Road
#05-10 Henderson Building
Singapore 0315

International Thomson Publishing Japan
Hirakawacho Kyowa Building, 3F
2-2-1 Hirakawacho
Chiyoda-ku, Tokyo 102, Japan

ISBN 0-534-51574-6

CONTENTS

INTRODUCT ION

This resource manual has been designed to assist instructors in using Samovar and Porter's *Intercultural Communication: A Reader,* Eighth Edition. Suggestions for organizing the course are offered as well as a description of chapter resources. Instructional Aids include sample course schedules for both quarter and semester systems, pedagogical suggestions for leading class discussions, four types of instructional resources for each of the text's eight chapters, and a number of film and video resources accompanied by one-sentence descriptions.

ORGANIZING THE COURSE

There are a number of ways to set up a college-level intercultural communication course. Some instructors use a culture-specific approach, where the commnicative behavior of one or more specific cultures are studied. Other instructors follow a culture-general approach, where the influence of culture on the communication process is explored as it applies to nearly all cultures. There are also courses that emphasize specifically the psychological, sociological, or linguistic influences on intercultural communication. Some intercultural communication college courses are similar to intercultural training workshops because they emphasize experimental simulation and role-playing activities designed primarily to increase student's cultural sensitivity and intercultural communication competence. *Intercultural Communication: A Reader* provides a set of readings that would complement any one or combination of these approaches. The diversity of the articles provides instructors with enough flexibility to teach a course in intercultural communication based on their own personal teaching style and approach to the subject.

CHAPTER RESOURCES

Each chapter of this instructors manual is divided into four sections: Chapter Synopsis, Discussion Questions, Exercises, and Test Items.

Chapter Synopsis
The chapter synopsis provides a summary of each article included in the text chapter. Special points of interests are identified and a description of how all the articles are linked in a given chapter is included.

Discussion Questions
Many instructors prefer to incorporate class discussion as a primary mode of instruction. Therefore, each chapter offers discussion questions for each article that will inspire students to talk about the readings.

Exercises
Activities can be particularly engaging for students in an intercultural communication course. They offer a change from the traditional university lecture by allowing students to demonstrate and experience concepts provided by the instructor or the course textbooks. Additionally, using

activities in the classroom is a powerful way to engage students in the course and in their own learning. Probably most important in the intercultural communication course is that activities transcend the classroom: "Instructional games, simulations, and role plays can enhance relevance of course material as students apply it in situations often designed to take them beyond the immediate classroom" (Nyquist & Wulff, 1990, p.350).

This manual offers a variety of instructional activities for each chapter of the text. The following is a description of each activity type and accompanying benefits.

1. *Role-Play: The* basic role play is a training activity where two participants (or more, though larger numbers are not common) take on characteristics of people other than themselves in order to attain a clearly defined objective. These "other people" -or roles - are usually fictitious, although they must be completely believable in the eyes of the training population for the role play to work. Participants who are not actively involved in the role play function as observers and look for certain things related to the overall objectives as the role play unfolds. (McCaffery, 1995, p.19)
    Benefits:
    -participants get a clear sense of identifiable skills in interpersonal situations, how they work, and the impact of things done effectively and ineffectively.
    -participants have an opportunity to feel what it is like to try out new or enhanced skills in real situations.
    -participants also get a chance to feel what it is like to be in another role. (p. 24)

2. *Simulation Games*: Simulation games provide interactive opportunities to practice new behaviors and experiment with new attitudes and points of view in a nonthreatening, nonjudgmental environment. They are particularly useful in intercultural training, since, in a very short time, they can stimulate cognitive and affective understanding and broaden participants' perspectives. (Sisk, 1995, p. 82)
    Benefits:
    -promotes critical thinking as participants analyze possible moves and probable consequences of those moves. Participants also must plan rationally and think through countermoves.
    -because chance is introduced, simulation games demonstrate that life is not always affected by logical plans or even intuitive solutions.
    -students learn on three levels: information, process, and strategies.
    -simulation games teach social values such as competition, cooperation, and empathy.
    -personal responsibility results when participants experience the way their decisions influence the future.
    -simulation games increase participants' knowledge and skills.
    -simulation games establish a sense of group dynamics and self awareness among participants. (p. 89).

3. *Critical Incidents*: Critical incidents are brief descriptions of situations in which there is a misunderstanding, problem, or conflict arising from cultural differences between interacting parties or where there is a problem of cross-cultural adaptation. Each

2

incident gives only enough information to set the stage, describe what happened, and possibly provide the feelings and reactions of the parties involved. It does not explain the cultural differences that the parties bring to the situation. These are discovered or revealed as a part of the exercise. (Wright, 1995, p. 128)
Benefits:
-increases participants' awareness of their own typical, idiosyncratic, or culturally determined interpretations and explanations of others' behavior and their own attitudes and responses in situations such as the ones described.
-draws out for comparison and analysis of various interpretations and perceptions of participants.
-clarifies the cultural differences in the incidents that might have contributed to the misunderstandings, problems, and conflicts.
-helps students behave more appropriately and effectively in similar situations. (p. 129)

4. *Culture Assimilator/ Intercultural Sensitizer*: "This instrument is specifically constructed to sensitize persons from one cultural group to the assumptions, behaviors, norms, perceptions, interpretations, attitudes, and values- in short, the subjective culture-of persons from another cultural group" (Triandis as cited in Albert 1995, p. 165).
Benefits:
-imparts knowledge of the subjective culture of the target group.
-helps participants develop more accurate expectations in intercultural interactions.
-helps participants interact more effectively with persons from the target culture.
-improves knowledge and application of cross-cultural communication concepts.
-increases participants' intercultural sensitivity. (p. 165)

5. *Case Studies*: "A case study is an account -usually written- of a realistic situation, including sufficient detail to make it possible for the participants in a training program to analyze the problems involved and to determine possible solutions" (Nadler as cited in Lacey & Trowbridge, 1995, p. 187). "A case study is to a critical incident what a simulation game is to a role play" (p. 187).
Benefits:
-reflects the actual complexities of cross-cultural interaction and illustrates that such situations are rarely as simple as they seem. It encourages participants to question the notion that there is one right way or one correct answer.
-It helps participants learn to weigh carefully the many factors which affect cross-cultural interaction and to avoid snap judgments which may have negative consequences for the trainee once on the job or in the field.
-It encourages students to learn from each other and to appreciate different opinions and is thus particularly effective in a group representing different cultures. (p. 193)

6. *Field Exercises*: Field exercises take the students outside the classroom to examine or experience the specified intercultural communication topic in real life.
Benefits:
-students increase their knowledge and behavior by experiencing the actual event outside the classroom.

-students get to experience members of other cultures.
-allows students the opportunity to practice the intercultural communication skills
   that they have learned in the classroom and from the textbook.
-helps students interact more effectively with members of other cultures.

7.   *Media Searches*: Media searches take students through all forms of media (papers,
   magazines, television, arts, etc.) to find examples of the specific concept.
   Benefits:
   -students learn the widespread nature of the cultural phenomenon.
   -students come to realize the cultural diversity of the world.
   -students realize the inevitability of cultural contact.
   -concepts are applied to the larger social setting and globalization.

The exercise section of each chapter offers an overarching activity that incorporates concepts and principles from each article in the chapter. This activity is particularly useful for instructors who do not have class time to accompany each article with an activity. The overarching activity is followed by activities that are designed to enhance each individual article. As a result, instructors who focus on select articles in certain chapters will have an activity specifically designed for those articles.

Test Items

Test items are included at the end of each chapter. Multiple choice, true/false, and essay questions are provided for constructing examinations.

INSTRUCTIONAL AIDS

SAMPLE COURSE SCHEDULES

It is common for instructors to use *Intercultural Communication: A Reader* in conjunction with another intercultural communication textbook. Although the reader can be used alone, undergraduate textbooks in intercultural communication can provide a comprehensive foundation for the study of culture, communication, and intercultural interaction. The course schedules provided on the following pages propose two organizational frameworks for using the *Reader* as the sole reading material in an intercultural communication course. They are intended only as guides and not as completed, ready-to-use course schedules. Your own course objectives, assignments, reading materials, and scheduling preferences must of course be considered when constructing a syllabus and course schedule.

If you are using a textbook in addition to the *Reader*, you will need to modify these frameworks accordingly. Because the course schedules provided include the use of every article in the *Reader*, these schedules will also need to be revised if you plan on using only selected articles. Weekly topic areas and corresponding readings and activities are provided for both a semester and quarter system. The course schedules were developed using the basic organization of the text's eight chapters: (1) Introduction, (2) U.S. Cultures and Intercultural Relationships, (3) International Cultures, (4) Verbal Processes, (5) Nonverbal Processes, (6) Context, (7) Improving Intercultural Communication and Relationships, and (8) Ethical Considerations.

Organization of a 10-Week, 30 Hour, 1-Quarter Course

Class Period	Content	Weekly Reading	Exercise
Week 1			
1	Introduction to the Course		
2	The Communication Process	Samovar/Porter	1.1,1.2
3	Why Study Intercultural Communication	Barnlund	1.3
	Culture and Identity	Collier	1.4
	Context and Meaning	Hall	1.5
Week 2			
4	Ethnic Identity	Martin	1.6
5	Ethnic Paradigms	Janzen	1.7
6	Confucianism & Relational Patterns	Yum	2.1,2.2
	Patterns in India	Jain/Kussman	2.3
	Arab Persuasion	Anderson	2.4
Week 3			
7	Maasai Patterns	Skow/Samovar	
	Greek Communication	Broome	2.5
8	Irish Conversations	Gannon	2.6
	Power and Intercultural Relations	Folb	3.1,3.2
9	African-American Communication	Ribeau, et al.	3.3
Week 4			
10	Communicating With Persons With Disabilities	Braithwaite	3.4
	Feminine and Masculine Cultures	Wood	3.5
11	Gay Culture in America	Majors	3.6
	The Elderly Co-Culture	McKay	3.7
12	Problem-Solving and Culture	Lieberman	4.1,4.2
Week 5			
13	Translations	Banks & Banks	4.3
	Idioms	Lee	4.4
14	Finnish Language Use	Carbaugh	4.5
	African-American Male Communication	Orbe	4.6
15	Language and Culture	Fong	4.7
	Mexican Proverbs	Zormeier/Samovar	4.8

Organization of a 15-Week, 45-Hour, 1-Semester Course

Class Period	Content	Weekly Reading	Exercise
Week 1			
1	Introduction to the Course		
2	The Communication Process	Samovar/Porter	1.1,1.2
3	Why Study Intercultural Communication	Barnlund	1.3
	Culture and Identity	Collier	1.4
Week 2			
4	Context and Meaning	Hall	1.5
5	Ethnic Identity	Martin	1.6
6	Ethnic Paradigms	Janzen	1.7
Week 3			
7	Confucianism & Relational Patterns	Yum	2.1,2.2
8	Patterns in India	Jain/Kussman	2.3
9	Arab Persuasion	Anderson	2.4
Week 4			
10	Maasai Patterns	Skow/Samovar	
11	Greek Communication	Broome	2.5
12	Irish Conversations	Gannon	2.6
Week 5			
13	Power and Intercultural Relations	Folb	3.1,3.2
14	African-American Communication	Ribeau, et al.	3.3
15	Communicating With Persons With Disabilities	Braithwaite	3.4
Week 6			
16	Feminine and Masculine Cultures	Wood	3.5
17	Gay Culture in America	Majors	3.6
18	The Elderly Co-Culture	McKay	3.7
Week 7			
19	Problem-Solving and Culture	Lieberman	4.1,4.2
20	Translations	Banks & Banks	4.3
21	Idioms	Lee	4.4

FILM AND VIDEO RESOURCES

This section includes several film and video titles that connect with and complement many of the articles in the *Reader*. With the literally thousands of titles available to instructors throughout the United States, you should be able to find several nonprint resources to enhance the reading and lecture material in your course. A short, one-sentence description is given for each title along with the year, publisher, and length of the film or video. Many of these titles have been viewed by the authors of this manual and several have been used by them a course in intercultural communication. We urge you to view those films and videos that you are interested in before showing them in your class. Other titles may be found by checking your own school's library reference section and media collection. In addition, several titles of film and video locators are provided to help you in your search for instructional media materials.

We encourage you to discuss each film with your students. Students should have an opportunity to talk about what they saw and heard so that concepts and ideas explored in readings, lectures, and exercises may be linked to each film.

VIDEO AND FILM TITLES

A Clash of Cultures, 1986, 60 min.: Explores African cultural adaptation to outside forces.

Across the Frontiers, 1977, 52 min.: Focuses on the influence of outside forces on tribal societies.

All Under Heaven: Life in a Chinese Village, 1986, 58 min.: Chinese language film (with subtitles) that tells of the history and life of one village in rural China.

American Tongues, 1987, 56 min.: Through interviews with U.S. Americans from many regions of the country, people discuss their attitudes and perceptions of theirs and others' speech.

America--Black and White, NBC, 1981, 75 min.: Through profiles of common citizens, details the serious social and economic situations of African Americans in the U.S.

Asianization of America, 1986, 26 min.: Explores the increasing influence of Asian immigrants to the United States, their influence on the American market, and negative stereotypes which Americans have had toward Asian immigrants.

Being Muslim in India, 1984, 41 min.: A family portrait of a Sunni Muslim and successful businessman in India.

Birthwrite: Growing Up Hispanic, 1989, 60 min.: Through interviews with Latino writers born or raised in the United States of Mexican and Puerto Rican parents, provides insight into the different worlds these writers experienced as children of a minority group.

Black on White, 1986, 58 min.: A film that explores the origins of black English and life in the U.S.

Brazil: Heart of South America, 1988, 55 min.:Basic introduction to the people of Brazil, including people of different social, ethnic, and geographic groups.

Bridging the Culture Gap, Copeland Griggs Productions, Inc., 302 23rd Ave., San Francisco, CA 94121 (415) 668-4200, 30 min.: Illustrates the contrasts between North American values and customs with those of cultures throughout the world.

Buddhism, MGHT, 1962, 16 min.: Compares the various sects and beliefs of Buddhism.

Bwana Toshi, ACI Films, II 5 min.: Problems encountered by a Japanese volunteer in Kenya.

Christians, Jews and Muslims in Medieval Spain, 1989, 52 min.: Traces the history of Christian, Jewish, and Muslim life in the Iberian peninsula from Roman times through Muslin conquest, through Chr*istian* reconquest. Emphasizes unique coexistence.

Communicating Across Cultures, Copeland Griggs Productions, 30 min.: Identifies several ways that culturally different individuals communicate; business context.

Communication: The Nonverbal Agenda, 1988, 20 min.: Discusses the influence that nonverbal cues can have on the meanings of our words.

Differences, Cinema Associates Productions Film, 25 min.: Individuals from different co-cultures relate the difficulties they experience with the dominant culture in the U.S.

Diversity at Work, Copeland Griggs Productions, 30 min.: Shows employees how to work and succeed in the multicultural organization.

Doing Business in Japan: Negotiating a Contract, 1976, 34 min.: Issues that impact the negotiation process (setting, language, interpreter) are examined.

Donahue: Street People, WGN, 1980, 45 min.: Interviews with several homeless people.

Ethnic Notions, 1987, 56 min.: A comprehensive, historical look at cultural stereotypes of African-Americans as portrayed through the U.S. media.

Eye of the Storm, CBS Television, 27 min.: Prejudice in a third grade classroom.

Faces of Change, American Universities Field Staff Films: Focuses on people around the world and their beliefs and values.

<u>Four Families</u>, MGHT, 1965, 60 min.: Focuses on how parents from different cultures raise and interact with their children.

<u>Four Religions</u>, MGHT, 1960, 60 min.: Discusses the beliefs of Hinduism, Buddhism, Islam, and Christianity.

<u>Gefilte Fish</u>, 1984, 15 min.: Cultural changes are represented as three generations of Jewish women prepare Gefilte fish, a traditional holiday dish.

<u>Hard Time</u>, Dave Bell Productions, 1980, 50 min.: Documents life in a maximum security prison.

<u>The Heritage of Slavery</u>, FA, 1968, 54 min.: Examines how the attitudes established during slavery still persist today.

<u>I Am not What You See: Being "Different" In America</u>, 1977, 28 min.: Documents the life of a woman with cerebral palsy who speaks about her experience as a disabled person in the U.S.

<u>I'isaw: Hopi Coyote Stories</u>, 1981, 28 Min.: The social group is represented in the Hopi Indians of Arizona who have been relatively successful in maintaining their land base, language, ceremonies, and cultural identity.

<u>Intercultural Contact</u>, Copeland Griggs Productions, 30 min.: Documents the effects of the Japanese presence in the U.S. through interviews with Japanese and U.S. citizens.

<u>Introduction to American Deaf Culture: Rules of Social Interaction</u>, 1985, 60 min.: Provides an introduction to social interaction among people who are deaf.

<u>Introduction to American Deaf Culture: Values</u>, 1986, 60 min. : Provides an introduction to the unique values and traditions of persons who are deaf.

<u>Invisible Barrier, The</u>, 1979, 18 min.: Examines the stereotype of the disabled including the discomfort of nondisabled persons who meet them for the first time.

<u>Language</u>, 1988, 55 min. (The Mind Series, Part 7): Explores different theories and ideas about the evolution of human language.

<u>Living Africa: A Village Experience</u>, 1983, 34 min.: Portrays the daily experiences and concerns of the people of Wassetake, a small village on the Senegal River in West Africa.

<u>Managing Differences</u>, Copeland Griggs Productions, 30 min.: Shows managers how to effectively work with a diverse work force.

Mentally Handicapped Children Growing Up: The Brooklands Experiment, 1968, 21 min. : Compares the development of children cared for in traditional institutions and small residential treatment programs.

The Five Pillars of Islam, 1988, 30 min.: Explains the major religious principles of Islam.

The Pinks and the Blues (Nova), WGHB, 1980, 57 min.: Discusses the socialization process that makes boys and girls "male" and "female."

The Primal Mind, 1983, 58 min.: Explores the basic differences between Native American and Western cultures.

Racism 101, 1988, 58 min.: Documents the racial tension that exploded on the University of Michigan campus after racist jokes were aired.

Radical Sex Styles, (ND), 44 min. : In six candid interviews, examines different approaches to human sexuality including lesbian, gay, bisexual, and transvestite perspectives.

Seven Minute Lesson: Acting as a Sighted Guide, (ND), 7 min.: A guide for sighted people to assist persons with visual impairments in everyday situations.

Sexes: What's the Difference?, 1978, 28 min. :Addresses the question of whether or not traits considered "male" and "female" are genetically inherent or learned in childhood.

Taoism: A Question of Balance, Time-Life, 1977, 52 min.: Discusses the religious beliefs of the Taiwanese.

The Rice Ladle: The Changing Role of Women in Japan, 1981, 28 min.: Explores the changing roles of women in Japan.

The Turning Points, WPBT-TV, Miami, 1973, 29 min.: Discusses the phenomenon of growing old in youthful America.

Wages of Action, 1979, 47 min.: A description of life in a Hindu village and how the Hindu religion touches each aspect.

We're Moving Up: The Hispanic Migration, NBC, 1980, 81 min.: Discusses the population and socioeconomic changes of the Latino people; values, cultural characteristics, and historical information are addressed.

Women in a Changing World, American Universities Field Staff Films, 48 min.: Women from around the world discuss issues of global concern.

Working in the U.S.A., Copeland Griggs Productions, 30 min.: Describes the values and dynamics of the U.S. workplace.

<u>Yo Soy</u>, 1985, 60 min.: Documents the progress that Chicanos have made in politics, education, labor, and economic development in the past two decades.

OTHER RESOURCES: Film and Video Locators

<u>AID catalog of films.</u> Agency for Economic Development's Training Office, USAID Library, 1621 North Kent Street, Rosslyn, VA 22209. (Films on Third World and non-Western countries only.)

Cortes, C. E., & Campbell, L. G. (1979). <u>Race and ethnicity in the history of the Americas: A filmic approach.</u> Riverside, CA: Latin American Studies Program, University of California, Riverside, 92521.

<u>The educational film locator.</u> Consortium of University Film Center. (Available in major libraries.)

Tricontinental Film Center, Third World Cinema, P.O. Box 4430, Berkeley, CA. UNESCO Publications Centre, P.O. Box 433, New York, NY 100 1 6.

<u>The 1986 video source book,</u> National Video Clearinghouse, 100 Lafayette Drive, Syosset, NY 11791.

THE FOLLOWING SOURCES WERE VERY HELPFUL IN COMPILING THIS INFORMATION:
Asuncion-Lunde, N. C. (nd). <u>Intercultural communication: Teaching strategies, resources and materials.</u> Unpublished paper.

<u>Directory of selected resources</u> (1988). Portland, OR: Intercultural Communication Institute.

<u>Educational media collection</u> (1991). Seattle: Instructional Media Services, University of Washington.

Kohls, L. R., & Tyler, V. L. (1988). <u>Area studies resources.</u> Provo, UT: David M. Kennedy Center for International Studies, Brigham Young University.

Samovar, L. A., & Stefani, L. A. (November, 1995). <u>Teaching the intercultural communication course at the college and university level.</u> A short course conducted for the Speech Communication Association Convention, San Antonio, TX.

Samovar, L. A. , & Stefani, L. A. (November, 1994). <u>Teaching the intercultural communication course at the college and university level.</u> Short course conducted for the Speech Communication Association, New Orleans, LA.

14

Schmidt, W. V., Freeman, J. B., Samovar, L. A., Kim, Y. Y., & Dodd, C. H. (November, 1984). Teaching the college course: Intercultural communication. *A* workshop presented at the convention of the Speech Communication Association, Chicago.

Stevens, G. I. (1993). Videos for understanding diversity. Chicago: American Library Association.

REFERENCES

Albert, R. D. (1995). The intercultural sensitizer/cultural assimilator as a cross-cultural training method. In S. M. Fowler & M. G. Mumford (Eds.), Intercultural sourcebook: Cross-cultural Training Methods, Vol. 1. Yarmouth, Maine: Intercultural Press.

Artman, R. (1976). The Miami Intercultural Communication Workshop. In D. S. Hoopes (Ed.), Readings in intercultural communication: Vol. V --Intercultural Programming. Pittsburg: The Intercultural Communication Network.

Bloom, B. S. (1956). Taxonomy of educational objectives: Cognitive domain. New York: David McKay Co.

Brislin, R. W. (1994). individualism and Collectivism as the source of many specific cultural differences. In R. W. Brislin & T. Yoshida (Eds.), Improving intercultural interactions: Modules for cross-cultural training programs. London: Sage Publications.

Can Communicate in Marrieta Ohio. (1993 June 24). The Seattle Times, p. 8.

Collins, V. H. (1958). A second book of English idioms. London: Longmans, Green and Co.

Covert, A. (1978). Communication: People speak instructor's manual. New York: McGraw-Hill.

Cushner, K. (1994a). Cross-cultural training for adolescents and professionals who work with youth exchange programs. In R.W. Brislin & T. Yoshida (Eds.), Improving intercultural interactions: Modules for cross-cultural training programs. London: Sage Publications.

Cushner, K. (1994b). Preparing teachers for an intercultural context. In R. W. Brislin & T. Yoshida (Eds.), Improving intercultural interactions: Modules for cross-cultural training programs. London: Sage Publications.

De Leon, F. M., & Macdonald, S. (1992, June 28). Name power. Seattle Post-Intelligencer.

Feig, P., & Blair, J. G. (1975). There is a difference: Seventeen intercultural perspectives. Washington, DC: Meridian House International.

Goodman, N. R. (1994). Intercultural education at the university level: Teacher-student interaction. In R. W. Brislin & T. Yoshida (Eds.), <u>Improving intercultural interaction: Modules for cross-cultural training programs.</u> London: Sage Publications

Holm, J. A. (1982). <u>Dictionary of Bahamian English.</u> New York: Lexik House Publishers.

Hoopes, D.S., & Ventura, P. (1979). <u>Intercultural sourcebook: Cross-cultural training methodologies.</u> LaGrange Park, Il: Intercultural Network.

Jankowski, K. (1991). On communicating with deaf people. In L.A. Samovar & R.E. Porter (Eds.), <u>Intercultural communication: A reader</u> (6th ed.). Belmont, CA: Wadsworth.

Lacey, L. & Trowbridge, J. (1995). Using the case study as a training tool. In S. M. Fowler & M. G. Mumford (Eds.), <u>Intercultural sourcebook: Cross-cultural training methods, Vol. 1.</u> Yarmouth, Maine: Intercultural Press.

Leslau, C., & Leslau, W. (1985). <u>African Proverbs.</u> White Plains, NY: Peter Pauper Press.

Lord, E. (1965). <u>Examples of cross-cultural problems encountered by Americans working overseas: An instructor's handbook.</u> Alexandria, VA: Human Resources Research Organization.

McCaffery, J. A. (1995). The role play: A powerful but difficult training tool. In S. M. Fowler & M. G. Mumford (Eds.), <u>Intercultural sourcebook: Cross-cultural training methods, Vol. 1.</u> Yarmouth, Maine: Intercultural Press.

Mullavey-O'Byrne, C. (1994). Intercultural communication for health care professionals. In rR. W. Brislin & T. Yoshida (Eds.), <u>Improving intercultural interaction: Modules for cross-cultural training programs.</u> London: Sage Publications.

Nyquist, J. L. (1979). <u>The instructional discussion method.</u> Seattle: University of Washington.

Nyquist, J. L., & Wulff, D. H. (1990). Selected active leaming strategies. In J. Daly, G. Friedrich, & A. Vangelisti (Eds.), <u>Teaching communication: Methods, research, and theory.</u> Hillsdale, NJ: Lawrence Erlbaum.

Powell, B. (1995, November 6). Keep your profits. <u>Newsweek.</u> p.98.

Sisk, D. A. (1995). Simulation games as training tools. In S. M. Fowler & M. G. Mumford (Eds.), <u>Intercultural sourcebook: Cross-cultural training methods, Vol. 1.</u> Yarmouth, Maine: Intercultural Press.

Wright, A. R. (1995). The critical incident as a training tool. In S. M. Fowler & M. G. Mumford (Eds.), <u>Intercultural sourcebook: Cross-cultural training methods, Vol. 1.</u> Yarmouth, Maine: Intercultural Press.

Chapter 1
Approaches: Understanding Intercultural Communication

Chapter Synopsis

This chapter introduces the topic of intercultural communication and provides a spectrum of approaches to culture, communication, and interactions between cultures. Your students should be able to answer five broad questions about intercultural communication after reading the articles in this chapter: (1) What IS intercultural communication? (2) How do cultures differ communicatively? (3) What influences and impedes intercultural understanding? (4) What makes up cultural identities and cultural ways of speaking? (5) How do perception and context influence the process of communication, and how do cultures differ along these dimensions?

Samovar and Porter provide basic information about the communication process and the components of culture. This article acquaints students with the core ideas about the subject of intercultural communication. Barnlund's article explores the need for change in how we communicate with each other in the global village. This article succinctly describes why we should study intercultural communication, and what we must consider as we go about communicating with people who are culturally different. Especially useful to the study of intercultural communication will be his discussion of how human beings tend to be drawn to those who are similar, and his discussion on the need to be aware of the individual and cultural assumptions that shape our communication with others.

Collier's article on cultural identities explores what "culture" consists of and how it is that people come to identify with one or more cultural groups. This article will be useful in helping you integrate students' own cultural backgrounds and identities into course readings, assignments, and exercises. Hall's article focuses on the influence of context in forming the meanings of messages. Most illuminating in this article is his discussion of low- and high-context cultures. Hall's use of numerous examples will make clear to students how important contexting is to the communication process and how different context cues can affect intercultural communication.

Martin probes the issue of what it means to be white in the United States in the 21st century. She identifies three dialects involved in white identity: White identity is both invisible and real, a privilege and a liability, and both positive and negative. She describes how the dialectics are played out in our communication with others. Students come away with the understanding that our identities are both shaping and being shaped by our communication. Finally, Janzen's article identifies five different paradigms in which Americans in general define ethnic relations. Beginning with Traditional Eurocentric Racism and ending with Centered Pluralism, Janzen traces the history of Multiculturalism. This article clearly identifies the assumptions, values, and goals of each paradigm. Janzen challenges the students to pay particular attention to the philosophical positions and perceptions of the numerous representatives of Multiculturalism in order to understand how the different paradigms affect intercultural communication.

Discussion Ideas

1. Why should we study intercultural communication?
   a. Ask students to list spontaneously their reasons for taking an intercultural communication course. What do they hope to get out of the course? What are the benefits? Why even have such a course? List their responses on the chalkboard.
   b. Ask students give their answers, play the "devil's advocate" and encourage students to elaborate on their reasons. For example, a common response to why we should study intercultural communication is that it will increase intercultural understanding among peoples of the world and help people get along. One response to this answer is that not everyone wants to communicate with people who are culturally dissimilar and what really are the benefits of such interactions? Hasn't communication been known to strain rather than improve intercultural relations? Why can't we just stay in our own communities and communicate with the people who are like us? Such a response can spark further dialogue on the inevitability of intercultural contact (as Samovar & Porter and Barnlund make clear).
   c. Finally, ask students to give one way that their lives could change as a result of taking an intercultural communication course. How will they have changed their lives or ways of thinking and communicating with culturally dissimilar individuals after the course has ended? Encourage students to be specific about these changes and have them write the changes down on a card and refer back to them at the end of the term.

2. Isn't there such a thing as "fact" and "objective reality"? Is all perception really culturally and individually based? Or can we agree that many things about the world just *are?* This question gets at Barnlund's notion that people can perceive the "same" experience very differently.

3. Why isn't it enough to know lots of facts about a culture in order to understand that culture? Can't we learn about cultures by just learning pieces of information about how they live, dress, eat, pray, etc.? This question focuses on the need to learn what Barnlund calls the "rulebooks of meaning" that distinguish one culture from another. Ask students what they would deem as important to include in a "rulebook of meaning." What must we know about a culture's way of viewing the world and human relationships before we can say we understand what constitutes that culture's rulebook of meaning? And why does this information help us communicate with people in different cultures?

4. What does it mean to have an individual identity? What does it mean to have a cultural identity? How do these two things differ? Are they interrelated, interconnected? This

discussion can illuminate the connection between who we are as individuals and our culture.

    a. Ask students to identify five or six words that they feel best describe their personality.

    b. Then ask them to try to link these characteristics to one or more of the cultures with which they identify. Do they see any connections? Has their culture influenced the development of their self. If, for example, students say that they are friendly, would they also say that friendliness is important in their culture?

    c. Trying to link their self and their culture will be a challenging task for many students, and in many instances students will have purposefully taken on personality characteristics that are not upheld by the teachings of their culture. These revelations will also be important because there may be specific reasons why they did not wish to adopt certain cultural characteristics.

5.   With which cultures do you identify? Why these and not others? Where are your primary loyalties? That is, what cultural characteristics do you adhere to most strongly? Are there some that may be more representative of one culture than another? This discussion can help students define cultural identity and question why they connect more with one cultural identity than another. Students can discover that who they are is often a combination of membership in many cultural groups. They should consider their religion, race, gender, sexual orientation, age, etc. when discussing these questions.

6.   What does Martin mean when she says there are competing notions involved in white identity? (i.e., invisible and real, positive and negative, and privilege and liability) How do these competing notions get acted out in our communication? Have the norms for white identity always been the same? This discussion will help students realize how cultural identities are negotiated, co-created, reinforced, and challenged through communication.

7.   What are the differences between racial and ethnic identity? Why do many scholars now argue for more of a social approach to understanding race? How does this position influence communication and identity negotiation? This discussion will help students discover that race is a complex mix of social meanings, rather than something fixed, concrete, and objective. Further this discussion makes clear the idea that our identities are both shaping and being shaped by our communication.

8.   Using the Interethnic Relationships paradigm chart provided by Janzen as a starting point, have students identify historical antecedents that have caused a shift in the five categories across paradigms. This will help students understand that history, context, and situations affect perceptions of ethnic relations. From their experiences in school, work, and life in general, in which paradigm would they classify most Americans? Is there a majority? Is there a progressive trend toward adopting paradigm V? Will new paradigms emerge as current ones become inadequate? What might they be? How do these paradigms affect intercultural communication?

Exercises

Exercise 1.1: Interactional Rules. This exercise includes aspects from all the articles in Chapter 1. Specifically, it illustrates how communication is so strongly rule-governed and yet we follow these rules unconsciously. By taking part in a cross-cultural simulation activity, students will gain insight into the difficulty that arises when two culture-specific rule systems are used in an intercultural interaction. Divide the class into two groups, the Sopa culture and the Epa culture. Each group should receive handouts with culture-specific rules that will govern its behavior when it interacts with the other (rules are provided as handout 1:8 at the end of the exercise section). Give students the rules one class period before the day that the game is to be played. This will ensure that each student will be adequately prepared to take part in the simulation. Tell students not to share their group's rules with any member of the other group. The success of this game hinges on each team not being explicitly aware of the rules that govern the other group's behavior.

After students have been given adequate preparation time to learn the rules of their assigned cultures, have the two groups take part in a twenty-minute interaction session. You may set up a scene where the two groups will negotiate a business transaction or a party where there is both social and business conversation taking place. You could even provide some refreshments to make a party scene more realistic. Some students from the same culture may wish to pair up as a married couple, business partners, friends, students, or siblings. After the two cultures have interacted, have the students write for five minutes on the following questions: What specific behaviors of the other culture did you notice? What social rules do you think were governing these behaviors?

As with all cross-cultural simulations, a class discussion should follow. Students should come away from this discussion with an understanding of some of the cultural rules that guide their own daily interactions and the impact that interactional rules have on intercultural communication. Each of the articles in Chapter I is relevant to this exercise. Some possible questions to stimulate discussion: What were some of the difficulties you experienced in preparing for this interaction? Which rules of your "adopted culture" conflicted with the rules of your "true" culture? When did you begin to catch on to some of their social rules? What was one of the first things you noticed about how the other culture behaved? What was your initial internal reaction? What was your external reaction to this behavior? How did you (or why didn't you) modify your behavior to compensate for the other culture's rules? What were some of the most difficult moments during your interactions? What were some of the most enjoyable? Did successful communication take place? What information about the other culture do you wish you had been given before your interaction? What information about your own culture could be given to other cultures to aid them in their interactions with you?

Exercise 1.1: Interactional Rules

Rules for the Sopa Culture

Sopas are extremely social, but their socializing is dictated by the women. Men can speak freely with other men, but must be restrained in contact with women. This matriarchal society is also highly materialistic. A major source of conversation is derived from discussing each other's material assets.

Example of greeting: Hi Jimmy! How's your new radial tire?

Keep in mind the following social rules:

A.   **Initiating Conversation.** Always begin social contact with materialistic statement. Inquiries into each other's financial situation is considered proper etiquette.

B.   **Degree of Verbalization.** Constant verbalizing is a sign of successful communication. Perpetual chitchat is critical both in social and business interactions.

C.   **Sex Roles.** Women must remember to protect their males from strangers. If a stranger stands too close to a male member, intercept without speaking.

D.   **Nonverbal Behavior.**

Touching: Each touches the other, except handshaking is considered an insult. Men must wait to be touched by women before they can reciprocate.

Gestures: The right hand is considered an evil and disgusting part of the human anatomy. It must never contact a human or be used in giving something to another. Right palm facing a person is an obscene gesture.

Eye Contact: Women engage in sustained eye contact. Men lower their eyes when speaking to women or strangers.

Facial Gestures. Wetting one's lips with the tongue is considered a very provocative or complimentary gesture to be used ONLY when one wishes to "charm" the opposite sex. Tongue rolling is a definite attempt at hustling. (gestures can be used by both sexes)

E.   **Business.** This highly materialistic society thinks of business as merely an extension of their social life, only more aggressive. Although men can initiate a sale, ONLY WOMEN CAN BARTER and complete the transaction.

Exercise 1.1: Interactional Rules

Rules for the Epa Culture

Epas believe in the separateness of the self from others. If possible, they would live in isolated cells, but since they form a group, they make all attempts to cooperate while minimizing self-revelation. Epas are themselves only part of the natural cycle and, therefore, hold nature as sacred as humans. They speak *through* nature so all communication is a metaphor.

Example: This rose is wilting. (I am tired.)
                Does the cow sit at your table? (Do you eat meat?)
                How are the saplings in your forest? (How is your family?)

Keep in mind the following social rules:

A. **Initiating Conversation.** Always begin social contact with reference to the weather or other natural phenomena.

B. **Degree of Verbalization.** The ability to use metaphorical language is an art form that establishes a type of caste system. Clear, moderately slow speech production punctuated with intermittent silence to enable aesthetic appreciation is a sign of articulate communication.

C. **Sex Roles.** Within the culture an asexual attitude prevails. Members tend to find other cultures very exciting but the treatment of sex and "nature's function" is sometimes misunderstood by strangers.

D. **Nonverbal Behavior.**

   Touching: Epas are essentially aphysical and, therefore, avoid touching one another. An interesting feature in this culture is that individuals seem to touch and hold themselves (i.e., arm folding, face touching, etc.) a lot. Positive sentiment is expressed in flowery metaphorical language.

   Gestures: Yes/agreement/happiness -- signified by touching chin to chest (rapid chin touching = great excitement/vigorous agreement). No/disagreement/disgust-rolling the shoulders. "Say again" or repeat--is indicated by touching your fist to your forehead.

   Facial Gestures: The human tongue is considered a disgusting part of the human anatomy. Showing your tongue or pointing a finger are considered GRAVE insults.

E. **Business.** The following only relate to business negotiations:

   1. All trading is done standing.
   2. Women cannot touch money.

Exercise 1.2: Intercultural Communication Model. This exercise corresponds with Samovar and Porter's introduction to intercultural communication. It asks students to construct their own model of the intercultural communication process based on those elements they feel most influence an intercultural interaction. Students will apply the knowledge they have learned in Chapter I to their own experiences as intercultural communicators. Briefly review the elements of intercultural communication as outlined in the article by Samovar and Porter. Then divide the class into groups of four to six students. Ask students to illustrate intercultural communication by constructing a model of the process (Samovar and Porter provide an example). Each group should decide which elements of intercultural communication they will include in their model. Suggest to the students that they use their own interactions with culturally different peoples as frameworks for choosing their model's components. For example, some students may have experienced an intercultural situation where language was a barrier in the interaction. Others may have noticed particular nonverbal behaviors that were markedly different than their own. Also stress to students that they should think of the basic process of communication discussed in the Samovar and Porter article while constructing their models.

Ask each group to present its model using a hypothetical intercultural interaction as an example that shows how the model works in "real life." If students are given enough time, some groups may choose to develop a skit to illustrate their model. Each group should state the respective cultures of the interactants, the scene (in a restaurant, on a date, in a classroom, etc.), and the affiliation level of the dyad (strangers, acquaintances, friends, lovers, etc.). The following questions are offered to stimulate discussion. How did you come up with these components? Which components do you feel most impact intercultural communication? Why? Which components do you feel pose the most trouble for interactants? The least trouble? Using the ingredients of communication listed by Samovar and Porter in Chapter 1, how are the components affected by the added variable of culture? Can any component escape culture's influence?

Exercise 1.3: Then and Now. This activity can be used with Barnlund's article on communication in the global village and illustrates the changing nature of a society. Divide the class into groups of four to five students. Have each group generate a list of objects, ideas, products, slogans, norms, and values that they or their parents encountered in the 1950s and 60s. Have each group then generate a similar list for the 1980s and 90s. You may wish to have students interview their parents or other people who grew up in a different generation than their own before taking part in this exercise. Ask students to draw parallels between the two lists: What has changed? What is no longer evident in today's society? Why have these changes occurred? How have these changes influenced people's lives? Students should discuss how these changes have affected relations between people from different ethnic, sexual orientation, gender, religious, and socioeconomic backgrounds. Ask students also to make some predictions about the 1990s: What's ahead for U.S. society? An open classroom discussion can follow with each group reporting their results to the class. The instructor or another student should use the chalkboard to record all of the answers.

Exercise 1.4: Identity, Race, and Culture. This exercise corresponds with the articles on cultural identity by Collier and Martin. It helps answer the questions, "Who am I?" and "Who are you?" Understanding the intercultural relationships that we enter into must start first with answering these two questions. This activity asks students to answer questions about their identity as a member of a certain cultural and racial group and then to interview someone as a member of his or her culture and race.

Ask students to answer each of the questions on the following page. It is important that students understand the difference between "culture" and "race" in order to do this exercise. Have students ask a friend or acquaintance to answer the questionnaire. The people they choose should be from a different cultural or racial group than themselves. Some questions will be ones that students may have never considered. Emphasize that they should try to answer them to the best of their abilities. Students should be informed that it might be wise to allow the people they are interviewing to complete the questionnaire by themselves so that they have ample time to consider their responses.

After students have completed both interviews, ask them to consider the questions that follow the questionnaire. These questions can be considered before they return to class or serve as questions for discussion during class time. Encourage students to talk with the person they interviewed about the questionnaire.

Ask students to consider some of the following questions. Was it difficult for you or your friend to complete certain portions of this questionnaire? Which parts and why? What differences do you see between the two sets of responses? What similarities? How do you explain the differences? How might these differences in cultural and racial identity affect an intercultural interaction or relationship?

Exercise 1:4: Identity, Race, and Culture

1. ; your culture mean to you?

2. .... it culture(s) do you identify? Do you identify more strongly with one culture than another? If yes, please explain.

3. What did you learn about your culture from your family?

4. How is your culture connected to your race?

5. What race are you?

6. Of what race do most people identify you as being a member?

7. How does it feet to be identified that way?

8. When were you first aware of your racial identity?

9. What did you learn about being a person of your race?

10. Have you ever wished you could be of a different race? If so, which race and why?

11. If you had been born into this racial group, how would you be different?

12. Of what are people of your race proud?

13. Ashamed of?

Exercise 1.5: Ranking Our Values. This exercise is an accompaniment for Hall's article on context and meaning. As Hall points out, quite often the influence of preprogrammed contexting (experience) or innate contexting (which is built in) is brushed aside. The same is true for values. Although we use our own cultural values every day when making decisions, we are usually not conscious of values as powerful guiding forces in our lives. Knowing our values can help us understand why we make the choices we do. Similarly, knowing the values of friends and acquaintances who are culturally different can provide insight into the choices they make.

This exercise asks students to reflect first on their own cultural values and then to ask a friend from a different cultural background to do the same. Students will complete the first part of this exercise outside of class. They are first to take the following list of values and rank them 1 through 10 according to their importance. Then students are to take the same list of values to a friend or acquaintance from a different culture and ask him or her to engage in the same ranking process. Students should make an "eyeball" comparison of their rankings with those of the person they asked to be a part of the exercise.

	Value	Rank
1.	individuality	
2.	work	
3.	freedom	
4.	leisure	
5.	friendship	
6.	health	
7.	family	
8.	equality	
9.	security	
10.	social acceptance	
11.	interpersonal harmony	
12.	efficiency	

The second part of this exercise may also be conducted outside of class or as an in-class discussion activity. Ask students to consider how differences in ranking of each of these values ct interpersonal intercultural interactions with others. What if equality is not high on ...ut a coworker lists it as the number one value for themselves? How would such differences affect your working relationship? How might differences in the values placed on individuality and family influence an intercultural relationship? If you value productivity and efficiency on the job and rate leisure as a less important value than work, how might you interact with a bank teller in another country who comes from a culture that tends to value leisure time and interpersonal harmony above work and for whom productivity is not a high priority? Can you describe a time when it was obvious that your values clashed with those of another individual? What happened and how did you resolve the value conflict? How can ethnocentrism manifest itself during an interpersonal interaction between people with value differences?

Exercise1.6: Philosophical Positions, Perceptions, and intercultural communication. This exercise will help the students better understand the five paradigms identified by Janzen and how they affect perceptions and intercultural communication. Divide the students into groups of two or three and have them pick a paradigm they are interested in. Have them first identify one or more underlying assumption(s) of the paradigm. Next have them interview five people regarding the assumption(s). For example, an underlying assumption of Centered Pluralism is that in order for America to hold itself together as a national system, there must be certain central traditions that are adhered to by most citizens. Interview five people and ask them what common traditions (if any) there should be for all Americans. Finally, students can report their findings as well as their own views to the rest of the class incorporating the impact on intercultural communication.

Test Items For Chapter 1

Multiple Choice

1. According to Porter and Samovar, which of the following are NOT among the events that have led to the development of the global village?
   a. globalization of the economy
   b. changes in immigration patterns
   c. developments in communication technology
   d. increased intercultural understanding *

2. Improvements in communication technology have produced many effects worldwide. Which of the following effects is among the most significant to intercultural communication?
   a. immediacy of new communication technology *
   b. increased television watching and decreased interpersonal interactions
   c. tendency to objectify people
   d. stronger value of materialism worldwide

3. Before behaviors can become messages they must meet two requirements. First, they must be observed by someone. What is the second requirement?
   a. They must be communicated intentionally.
   b. They must be explicit.
   c. They must elicit a response. *
   d. They must be understood by the receiver.

4. According to Almaney and Alwan (1982), what are the three categories or elements that define "culture"?
   a. thought, language, and action
   b. artifacts, concepts, and behaviors *
   c. reason, emotion, and credibility
   d. emblems, ideas, and experiences

5. The women's movement in the United States best exemplifies which of the following characteristics of culture?
   a. selectivity
   b. ethnocentrism
   c. transmissibility
   d. interrelatedness of facets *

6. Which of the following is NOT a major sociocultural influence on the development of our perceptions?
   a. race *
   b. beliefs, values, and attitudes
   c. world view
   d. social organizations

7. Culture is
   a. static.
   b. innate.
   c. random.
   d. learned. *

8. What are the two dominant social organizations found in a culture?
   a. political affiliation and club memberships
   b. workplace and peer group
   c. school and family *
   d. ethnicity and community identification

9. Silence, eye contact, and handshakes are all forms of what kind of communication?
   a. nonverbal *
   b. paralinguistic
   c. conscious
   d. intentional

10. According to the scale of Minimum to Maximum Socio-cultural differences, which of the following pairs of groups would one expect to find the least number of diverse cultural factors?
    a. U.S. American-British
    b. Heterosexual-Homosexual *
    c. U.S. American-German
    d. Urban American-Rural American

11. Communication context refers to
    a. the people present.
    b. the social surroundings.
    c. the physical surroundings.
    d. the physical and social surroundings. *

12. According to Dean Barnlund, increasing physical proximity has accomplished which of the following among the world's people?
    a. intensify divisions *
    b. broaden cultural understanding
    c. decrease ethnocentrism
    d. increase intimacy

13. "The People" refers to a self-descriptive term often used by
    a. European cultures.
    b. African cultures.
    c. Asian cultures.
    d. many cultures throughout the world. *

14. "Interpersonal understanding" is a function of or is dependent upon the degree of the similarity of
    a. value, beliefs, and attitudes.
    b. perceptual orientations, systems of belief, and communicative styles. *
    c. ways of knowing and ways of communicating.
    d. world and personal views.

15. "Similarity in perceptual orientations" refers, in part, to how a person
    a. perceives of him- or herself in the world.
    b. defines the existence of humankind.
    c. approaches reality. *
    d. compares his or her own culture with other cultures.

16. Which of the following is *not* included in Barnlund's definition of "communicative style"?
    a. The sex of the individual. *
    b. The depth of involvement people demand of each other.
    c. The topics about which people choose to speak.
    d. The reliance on the same set of communication channels.

17. A culture's "universe of discourse" refers to
    a. its particularized and idiosyncratic language used only by members.
    b. verbal and nonverbal elements of communication in their entirety used by a particular community, group , or culture.
    c. the belief that all cultures are constructed and maintained through communication.
    d. a way in which people can interpret and convey their experiences to each other. *

18. How does Collier define culture?
    a. Rules for appropriate conduct and living in a given community.
    b. An historically transmitted system of symbols, meanings, and norms. *
    c. The deposit of knowledge, experience, beliefs, values, and attitudes acquired by a group of people in the course of generations through individual and group striving.
    d. A particular and idiosyncratic way of perceiving the world.

19. According to Collier, which of the following is the basis with which a group may define itself as a culture?
    a. gender
    b. geographical area
    c. organization
    d. all of the above *

20. While a social psychological perspective of identity formation may view the self as centered in social roles and practices, a communication perspective emphasizes the _____ process in which messages are exchanged between persons.
    a. interactional
    b. transactional *
    c. behavioral
    d. active

21. Which of the following is *not* a property or characteristic of cultural identities?
    a. content and relationship levels of interpretation
    b. scope and form of identity
    c. mode of expression
    d. none of the above *

22. *While ascription* refers to how others view our identities ("This is who you are"), the process of *avowal* is best exemplified in which of the following statements?
    a. "This is who I think I am."
    b. "This is who I am to YOU."
    c. "This is who I am." *
    d. "This is who I think you think I am."

23. Authenticity, powerlessness, and expressiveness were identified as three _____ of African-Americans in a study exploring this culture's perspectives on interethnic communication.
    a. core symbols *
    b. labels
    c. attitudes
    d. value signifiers

24. When Mexican-Americans speak Spanish in their own neighborhood communities, which property or characteristic of cultural identity formation is being enacted?
    a. ascription and avowal
    b. content and relationship levels of interpretation *
    c. scope and form of identity
    d. affective, cognitive, and behavioral components

25. The rules governing what one perceives include taking into account which of the following?
    a. culture
    b. social status
    c. past experience
    d. all of the above *

26. According to Barnlund, when judges and juries in U.S. court systems concern themselves with only "the law" and what is legally part of the record, they are most notably ignoring which of the following categories that govern perception?
    a. situation *
    b. subject
    c. past experience
    d. culture

27. What one pays attention to or does not attend to is largely a matter of
    a. intelligence.
    b. maturity.
    c. context. *
    d. interest level.

28. In high-context cultures, much time must be devoted to
    a. elaborate description.
    b. technical language.
    c. verbalization.
    d. programming. *

29. Bernstein's "restricted" code refers to language that
    a. is more distinct and precise.
    b. uses shortened sentences and merged sounds. *
    c. provides more words than are necessary.
    d. only cultural members understand.

30. To tell a person more than he or she needs to know is to _____ them.
    a. code-restrict
    b. code-reverse
    c. high-context
    d. low-context *

31. Contexting involves which of the following pairs of processes?
    a. explicit and implicit
    b. physiological and psychological
    c. internalized and situational *
    d. biological and emotional

32. According to Barnlund, what an animal perceives is dependent on status, activity, setting, and experience. What one dimension must we add when studying human perception and communication?
    a. language
    b. culture *
    c. religion
    d. political views

33. According to the Traditional Eurocentric Racism Paradigm (I):
    a. America was characterized by a dominant Orthodox Christian tradition.
    b. All Europeans, despite their religious affiliation, experienced no discrimination.
    c. Non-Europeans, such as American Indians, Blacks, Asians, and Mexicans, were all considered inferior peoples and were never fully accepted as Americans. *
    d. Protestant, Catholic, Christian, and Jewish religions were readily accepted.

34. Janzen indicates that in the melting pot paradigm (II):
   a. rather than melting equally into American society, immigrants had to shed their traditional cultural beliefs and practices in favor of "American" ones. *
   b. all immigrant groups retained their own languages.
   c. marrying across ethnic boundaries was prohibited.
   d. we find an accurate account of what actually transpired in American history.

35. Which paradigm advocates the creation and maintenance of semi-independent or separate ethnic groups within the U.S.?
   a. Globalism (IV)
   b. Ethnic Nationalism (III) *
   c. Central Pluralism (V)
   d. Traditional Eurocentric Racism (I)

36. According to Janzen:
   a. all five paradigms are present in todays society. *
   b. these five paradigms make solutions to social problems easier.
   c. it is easy to identify the "real" multiculturalists.
   d. the last three paradigms have leveled the playing field for most ethnic groups.

True/False

F	1.	The globalization of the economy has had little impact on intercultural communication among the world's people.
T	2.	Intercultural communication occurs whenever a message produced in one culture must be processed in another culture.
F	3.	Messages that are communicative must be sent intentionally and consciously.
T	4.	A basic function of culture is to help us make sense of our surroundings.
T	5.	The deep structure of a culture (i.e., values, morals, religious practices) rarely changes because it is able to resist major alterations.
F	6.	Culture is the internal process by which we select, evaluate, and organize stimuli from the external environment.
T	7.	Values are like rules that proscribe behaviors expected of a culture's members.
F	8.	More than anything else, differences in language isolate cultures and cause them to regard each other as strange.
T	9.	The "rulebooks of meaning" refer to those ways of perceiving the world that different cultures have.
F	10.	"Similarity in systems of belief" refers to the way people view the world.
T	11.	The interpersonal equation is based on the assumption that similar people are drawn to each other.
T	12.	According to Collier, we become members of groups, in part, by learning about past members of the group.

F	13.	All groups of people who define themselves as a unit are cultures.
T	14.	Only when a group develops a history and hands down the symbols and norms to new members can it be said to have a cultural identity.
F	15.	The term *amae* is a Japanese word meaning "self."
F	16.	The cognitive component of identity relates to the feelings we have about that identity.
T	17.	Our identities emerge and develop as we interact with people.
F	18.	Culture and communication are synonymous.
T	19.	A deep sense of culture need not be present for communication to take place.
T	20.	Meaning in communication is not complete without knowledge of the context.
F	21.	One's social status does not usually affect what an individual perceives and does not perceive.
F	22.	When using an elaborated code, a person need not be explicit or precise but rather can assume that a listener understands the message implicitly.
T	23.	In contrast to low-context communication, high-context communication tends to be fast and efficient.
T	24.	Our identities are negotiated, co-created, reinforced and challenged through communication.
T	25.	Many scholars now feel that racial categories are socially constructed.
F	26.	Cultural practices and norms that link white people are obvious and explicit.
T	27.	Bounded cultures, according to Martin, are those groups we belong to that are specific and not dominant or normative, such as religion, gender, and ethnicity.
T	28.	The Traditional Eurocentric paradigm (I) and the Melting Pot paradigm (II) are both assimilationist paradigms.
T	29.	The paradigms of Ethnic Nationalism (III), Globalism (IV), and Centered Pluralism (V), all seek the retention and maintenance of traditional cultural beliefs and practice.
F	30.	According to Centered Pluralism, all ethnicities contribute to a rapidly changing American character.
T	31.	Globalism asks us to think in terms of foundations that might hold all cultures of the world together.

Essay Questions

1. Identify and discuss the four major events that have led to the development of the global village.
2. Explain what is meant by the following phrase: "The difficulty with being thrust into a global village is that we do not yet know how to live like villagers; there are too many of us who do not want to live with 'them.'" In your essay, discuss your own view on this statement.
3. Discuss the implications of the following statement about communication: "Any behavior that elicits a response is a message."
4. Describe an intercultural communication interaction that you have experienced using the four

characteristics of communication as identified by Porter and Samovar.

5. Describe how the mechanisms of invention and diffusion produce change in a culture.

6. Identify, define, and give an example of each of the six characteristics of culture as explained by Porter and Samovar. Would you add a characteristic that they do not include?

7. Describe how beliefs, values, and attitudes are interrelated and their relation to communication.

8. Explain the model of intercultural communication as depicted by Porter and Samovar. How does the process of intercultural communication work?

9. What does Barnlund suggest is most critical for a global village to survive?

10. How is it that people can perceive the "same" experience so differently?

11. Explain the equation of "Interpersonal Understanding" given below. How does culture influence this equation? What happens to the process of interpersonal understanding when intercultural contact takes place?

Interpersonal Understanding = (similarity of perceptual orientations,
similarity of belief systems, similarity of
communicative styles)

12. What does Barnlund mean by the following statement: "It is when people nurtured in such different psychological worlds meet that differences in cultural perspectives and communicative codes may sabotage efforts to understand one another."

13. According to Barnlund, what are the dangers of the "individual unconscious" and the "cultural unconscious"? How can people break free of the "boundaries of their own experiential worlds" and communicate successfully with culturally different peoples?

14. Describe what Collier refers to as a "cultural identity." What makes up such an identity?

15. Give Collier's definition of culture and explain each part of the definition.

16. Describe how groups may go about defining themselves as cultures.

17. Briefly describe the properties that form cultural identities. Now apply these properties to your own cultural identity(ies). Can you describe your own cultural identity(ies) using Collier's characteristics?

18. How are cultural and intercultural competence different? How are they related?

19. What five categories provide rules that govern what a person perceives in the world?

20. Explain Hall's notion of low- and high-context messages. Describe two cultures that tend to be at the more extreme ends of Hall's context continuum.

21. How are Bernstein's restricted and elaborated codes similar to Hall's theory of low- and high-context messages?

22. Discuss Hall's notions of internalized/innate contexting and situational contexting. How are they interrelated to form a more holistic sense of "context"?

23. Martin suggests that "whiteness" becomes invisible in society. Explain what she means and how this invisibleness happens.

24. How might aspects of white identity influence communication with others?

25. Describe the primary differences between the Traditional Eurocentric Racism (I), Melting Pot (II) paradigms and the Ethnic Nationalism (III), Globalism (IV), Centered Pluralism (V) paradigms.

26. Explain why Janzen calls the Globalism (IV) paradigm a "Star Trek vision."
27. Describe the historical nature of culture as discussed by Samovar & Porter, and Collier. How do these authors support the statement, "Culture is historically transmitted"?
28. How do Collier and Martin describe the formation and enactment of cultural identity?
29. Several of the articles in Part One describe culture as selective. Using Barnlund's notion of the sources of meaning (i.e., some sort of structure must be placed upon the endless profusion of incoming signals) and Hall's notion of culture as a "highly selective screen between man and the outside world," describe how culture is selective.
30. Using information and examples from each of the articles in Part One of the *Reader*, describe how culture is like a "screen" that allows individuals to attend to only certain stimuli and ignore all others.
31. Using information from each of the articles in Part One, identify some of the ways culture is "subtle."
32. Using information from each of the articles in Part One, answer the following questions: What does it mean to communicate interculturally? What must people consider when they communicate interculturally?

Chapter 2
International Cultures: Understanding Diversity

Chapter Synopsis

Chapter 2 focuses on cultures around the world and how their world views and belief and value systems influence their communication. Students will be challenged with the following four questions about intercultural communication after reading this chapter: (1) What cultural differences exist between Eastern and Western peoples? (2) How do these differences influence their ways of communicating? (3) What are the different modes and methods of persuasion valued and practiced by different cultures? (4) How do different cultures conceive of interpersonal conflict and struggle, and why does conflict pervade the everyday lives of members of some cultures and be avoided at all costs in others?

June Ock Yum's article describes the influence that Confucianism has on the interpersonal relations in East Asia. Her article will be especially helpful to students in detailing how a major religion and philosophy profoundly influences how people in China, Korea, and Japan communicate and form relationships. Her discussion of East Asian and North American patterns of communication and relationship development details clearly the differences between these cultures. Jain and Kussman's article on Hindus in India is a comprehensive overview of the philosophy behind the Hindu way of life. Many preconceptions about the peoples of India abound. This article will be most instructive in informing students about the country of India and the pervasive influence of the Hindu religion on Indian life and communication.

Anderson uses a different method to illustrate important distinctions between Arab and American conceptions of persuasion. Students will be exposed to cultural communication as displayed in articles of two major U.S. newspapers. One of the most illuminating aspects of this article is Anderson's "line-by-line" rhetorical analysis of the impact of culture on persuasion. Students will understand how people from different cultures formulate persuasive arguments based on their own world views, beliefs, and ways of speaking. Broome's article describes the pervasiveness and acceptance of conflict and struggle in Greek interpersonal interaction. Students will learn that conflict isn't just accepted by Greek peoples but is expected and is a crucial force in the development of Greek interpersonal relationships.

Skow and Samovar provide details of the Maasai culture. They trace the history, values, and worldview of this African culture that has shunned all Western influence. A discussion of Maasai verbal and nonverbal processes show the impact of culture on communication. Finally, Gannon's article uses the characteristic or metaphor of Irish conversations to illustrate the importance of language for Irish people. Through an examination of worldview and history, Gannon traces the Irish antecedents for their great pride in language. He describes the influence of language on Irish culture and the implications for day-to-day life.

These articles will help the students understand that members from different cultures bring different histories and worldviews to the communication event and these differences impact and influence the interaction.

Discussion Ideas

1. How would relationship development differ among people who value *being* versus *doing?* Ask students to describe a person who values a "being" perspective of life and one who values a "doing" perspective. Are such persons so different that they could not form a satisfying interpersonal relationship or communicate effectively?

2. Confucian philosophy makes a strong distinction between in-group and out-group members. What influence might this distinction have on intercultural interactions?
   a. Ask students to first describe this distinction between in-group and out-group members. How are the Confucian concepts of *jen, i,* and *li* related to this distinction?
   b. Then ask students to consider a scenario where followers of Confucianism and followers of a culture where in-group/out-group distinctions are not strong are communicating. What problems may arise? What assumptions may each group hold of the other?
   c. Now ask them to consider how these two groups might be able to communicate and work together even though they may have very different views of "groupness."

3. What kind of communication would ensue between a person who has a process, receiver view of communication and a person who has an outcome, sender view of communication? What are the differences in perception that these two people must overcome if they are to communicate effectively? Is it enough just to know that each has a different view of communication or must adjustments be made? (This raises the issue of whether "just knowing" about differences in communication is enough. Usually it is not.) If adjustments need to be made, ask students to consider what those adjustments might be.

4. How would the Hindu view of life, the world, and salvation influence communication between Hindus and non-Hindus?
   a. Ask students to first describe in their own words the various beliefs of the Hindu religion. Record their responses on the chalkboard by labeling separate columns as "life," "world," and "salvation."
   b. Next, ask them to take another culture that they have read about (the Greeks or Chinese, for example) and describe how people from these cultures would view these same three topics.
   c. With the two sets of cultural beliefs on the board, ask students to reflect on how two people from these two -cultures might communicate differently.

5. How are the Greek notion of in-groups and out-groups related to the Confucian principle of *jen* and the Hindu caste system?

6. What qualities best describe and distinguish the Arab and American forms of persuasion? Engage students in this discussion by listing the qualities they generate side by side on the chalkboard. Given these two lists, what can each group do to convince the other? Is successful communication impossible when two parties are coming from such different ways of persuading? Is there any "common ground" for Arabs and Americans to use to negotiate? Does one "give in" to the other side by using persuasion that is more culturally appropriate and acceptable to one's audience?

7. How has the Maasai rejection of much of the culture of the West affected the perceptions of them by the government and other tribes? How might these perceptions further complicate communication?

8. How does the Irish notion of conversation differ from that of North Americans and how might these differences influence intercultural interaction?

Exercises

Exercise 2.1: Success Across Nations. This exercise ties into all the readings in Chapter 2 by having the students expand their definition of what it means to be successful. Having read about the values and culture of people from Chinese, India, Saudi Arabia, Africa, Ireland, and Greece, it asks the students to do two things. First, it asks the students identify what success means to them. After evaluating their own definition of success, they will attempt to define what it means to be successful if you are a member of the 6 cultures examined in Chapter 2. So what is a successful Chinese, Indian, Saudi Arabian, Maasai, Irish, or Greek man? Woman? Child?

The second part of this exercise will give students experience interacting with people who may come from different cultural backgrounds than their own. As a basis of comparison between their own definition of success and the definitions of success based on the 6 cultures examined, ask the students to contact one to three people who did not grow up in the U.S. Students should interview each person and determine how each defines success and how each would describe themselves as a successful person. Some of the questions below will help students come up with their own definition, analyze the definitions of the 6 cultures, and conduct interviews with others:

1. How would you define a successful person?
2. How would you define the typical or "traditional" notion of a successful person?
3. Would you say that you are a successful person? Why or why not?
4. How does your success differ from the "traditional" notion of success?
5. How have the people in your life (family, friends, coworkers, spouse, etc.) influenced your success?

6. What problems have arisen for you in your work? What barriers have you had to overcome in order to be a successful person?
7. Have there been any problems relating or interacting with people that have influenced you negatively or positively as you became a successful person?
8. Has interacting with people from different countries and cultures had an impact on your success?

Ask students to write up the findings and compare them with other members of the class.

Exercise 2.2: Living with Intercultural Communication. This exercise can be used when studying the Yum article. This case study illustrates what happens when two ways of perceiving, communicating, and living conflict. It is also about what can happen when people assume that those around them adopt the same way of living and can understand their ways of communicating. Have students read the case study below and answer the questions that follow. As students read, ask them to consider what assumptions are being made by Michelle and Tomiko as they work through their situation.

It was the first week of school and Michelle and Tomiko were getting along very well as new roommates. Michelle was an African-American junior and Tomiko was an exchange student from Japan. They were both studying international business and took one class together. Both had busy schedules and usually ate meals separately. Although she thought it was very kind of Tomiko, Michelle didn't feel comfortable when Tomiko would do Michelle's breakfast dishes for her. She was used to living with people who cleaned up after themselves. She asked Tomiko to just leave them and she would do them when she got home in the evening. But Tomiko continued to wash Michelle's dishes, saying that she really didn't mind.

After about a month, Michelle noticed that something was bothering Tomiko. She rarely spoke to Michelle in the morning before they went to school and would walk out of the kitchen or living - room when Michelle entered. Feeling very uncomfortable, Michelle finally asked Tomiko what was wrong. Tomiko was surprised that Michelle didn't already know. As it turns out, Tomiko had become frustrated that although she did Michelle's breakfast dishes, Michelle almost never did Tomiko's dinner dishes. Michelle didn't understand why Tomiko hadn't brought this up with her before. Tomiko said she figured Michelle understood what was troubling her without telling her.

"Although I appreciate it, I remember telling you that I'd prefer if you just left my dishes until I returned in the evening. I'm used to doing only my own dishes."

"I don't see a difference between my dishes and yours. They are the same.

"I guess I'm just used to people doing their own. You know, we all get busy and I just have time to do my own dishes."

"But if we do each other's then it all works out."

Their conversation ended soon after and Michelle realized things were still not settled. She respected Tomiko's view of living with another person but wasn't sure how much of her view she could adopt. One of the reasons Michelle rarely cooked was because she didn't like to clean up afterward, They would both need to discuss the issue some more.

Some questions to spark class discussion: What were the two competing views of communal living evident in this case study? Which view most resonates with your notion of communal living? How do you think your culture, or more specifically, your family upbringing and expectations of roommates, have influenced this view? What assumptions were made by Tomiko and Michelle in the scenario? How did these assumptions affect their conversation? How does the notion of contexting" connect with this scene? If you had this same situation with a roommate, what would you do to improve relations between Michelle and Tomiko? Have you ever encountered a situation in which you were looking at something from a different angle or perspective than another person? Did cultural differences play a role in the conflict?

Exercise 2.3: Values that Conflict and Correspond. This exercise can be used in conjunction with the Jain and Kussman article, Dominant Cultural Patterns of Hindus in India. This activity asks the students to consider what they value in life and make value comparisons between Indians as presented in the chapter, themselves, and a friend or acquaintance from a different cultural background. After reading the article, students can rank cultural values by using the value inventory scale on the next page. Students can use a scale of 1 (most valued) to 10 (least valued). After ranking the values for the Indian culture from the reading and ranking themselves, students are to ask a person from another country to rank the items.

Have the students report their findings to the class. Use some of the following questions to discuss students' responses. What were the five top values of the Indian culture? The top values that you ranked and the five top values of your friend? What differences and similarities are there? How do these rankings reflect the values of your cultures? What are some examples of how the Indian culture as well as you and your friend's culture have "taught" you to value certain things in life? What values, if any, were not on the list that you and/or your friend and/or a member of the Indian culture believe should have been included? How might differences in cultural values influence interpersonal interactions? How might such differences lead to interpersonal conflict? How much do similarities and differences in values enhance intercultural communication? What value differences might be insurmountable? Which would be incidental?

Exercise 2.3: Values that Conflict and Correspond

Value Inventory

Rank the following list of values from 1 (most valued) to 10 (least valued). Use column A to record predicted Indian responses. Use column B to record your responses. Then ask a person from another country to rank the items and record them in column Cs. The definitions provided after each value are not meant to be definitive meanings. They are to allow you and your friend to complete this inventory using the same definitions for each value.

	Value	A	B	C
1.	Happiness (contentedness)	___	___	___
2.	Freedom (independence, free choice)	___	___	___
3.	Salvation (being saved, eternal life)	___	___	___
4.	Family security (taking care of loved ones)	___	___	___
5.	Self-respect (self-esteem)	___	___	___
6.	Equality (sister- /brotherhood, equal opportunity)	___	___	___
7.	Sense of accomplishment (making a lasting contribution)	___	___	___
8.	A world at peace (free of war and international conflict)	___	___	___
9.	Wisdom (a mature understanding of life)	___	___	___
10.	A comfortable life (a prosperous life)			

Value Comparison

Predicted Top Values of India	My Top Values	My Friend's Top Values
_____	_____	_____
_____	_____	_____
_____	_____	_____
_____	_____	_____
_____	_____	_____
_____	_____	_____
_____	_____	_____
_____	_____	_____
_____	_____	_____

Exercise 2.4: Truism and Arguments. We have seen in the Anderson article comparing Arab and American concepts of effective persuasion that the truism of one nation becomes an argument for another. This article clearly exemplifies how cultural contact can often result in misunderstandings and conflict. This exercise asks the students to find an analogous situation in current events. Divide the students into groups of 3 or 4. Each group will then search newspapers, news magazines, news channels, etc. and find a current or ongoing event involving two cultures. For example, the recent Diawa Bank scandal, Bosnia, Human Rights issues in China, etc. After thoroughly investigating the issue, students are to prepare a summary to be presented to the class of how culture has impacted or may impact the situation. For example, the Anderson article focused on concepts of effective persuasion through cultural orientations to discourse and the historical context of culture.

The following are some questions the students might want to include as part of their summaries:

- What framing devices are being used by both cultures? For example, portrayal as victims, aggressors, innocent by-standers, etc.

- What organizational principles are being employed by each side? For example, organization by fact, logical or chronological sequences, linear or circular sequences, historical context, overarching issues, etc.

- What justifications are involved from each culture?

- How does language impact the situation?

- What cultural values are exemplified in each culture's stance?

- Is there evidence that either culture is attempting to understand the other's values?

- What are your recommendations for improved interaction in this situation?

Exercise 2.5: Showing Our Feelings. In some cultures, the expression of anger by yelling and cursing may be acceptable. In others, it would be considered quite inappropriate. The extent to which we reveal ourselves through laughter, tears, anger, anxiousness, and jealousy depends in large part on how our families and communities displayed emotions and when we were chastised or rewarded as children for emoting inappropriately or appropriately. We learned from culture how to show and not show our feelings.

This exercise focuses on how often and intensely we show our emotions and how we feel when others express their emotions. This exercise is designed to help students understand more about their own emotional responses so that they might be in a better position to begin to understand how and why other cultures use emotion during interpersonal conversations. This exercise may be used in conjunction with Broome's article on styles of discourse among Greek peoples.

Ask students to respond to the list of emotions provided as a handout on the next page by indicating from 1 to 6 how often they express these emotions and how comfortable they feel when others express them. Use the scales below to rate each emotion. The blank line at the end of the list is for you or your students to fill in if you or they wish to add any emotions to the list.

After asking students to complete this list, ask them to consider the following questions. Which emotions do you have the least/most difficulty expressing and why? Which emotions do you have the least/most difficulty watching others express and why? Which discrepancies, if any, are there between the extent to which you are willing to show certain emotions and your feelings of comfort watching others express the same emotion? Think of Broome's example of how Greek interactions are intense, combative, and loud and how this behavior is appropriate and acceptable in Greece. How do you think your expression of emotions and your responses to others' emotions have been influenced by cultural beliefs and attitudes? What differences and similarities are there in the displaying of emotions among your friends or classmates who come from different cultural backgrounds? How might intercultural communication be influenced by such differences?

Exercise 2.5: **Showing Our Feelings**

Displaying Your Emotions   Watching Others' Emotions

1 very frequently   1 very comfortable
2 frequently   2 comfortable
3 occasionally   3 somewhat comfortable
4 not very often   4 not very comfortable
5 rarely   5 uncomfortable
6 never   6 very uncomfortable

Displaying Your Emotions		Watching Others' Emotions
_____	angry	_____
_____	loving	_____
_____	concerned	_____
_____	anxious	_____
_____	confident	_____
_____	sad	_____
_____	depressed	_____
_____	jealous	_____
_____	insecure	_____
_____	silly	_____
_____	violent	_____
_____	argumentative	_____
_____	proud	_____
_____	friendly	_____
_____	playful	_____
_____	envious	_____
_____	belligerent	_____
_____	flirtatious	_____
_____	hostile	_____
_____	guilty	_____
_____	unsure	_____
_____	impatient	_____
_____	arrogant	_____

Exercise 2.6: Irish and Greeks Unite Through the Broome and Gannon articles we have seen how forms of communication can vary widely from culture to culture. We learned from this chapter that increased intercultural interaction has the potential for misunderstandings as well as conflict. This role play has the students take on the language characteristics typical of the Greeks and Irish. Divide the class into groups of 4 to 5 students. Assign 2 or more groups to "become Greek" and 2 or more groups to "become Irish." Each student is to become thoroughly familiar with his or her assigned cultural language characteristics as relayed by Broome and Gannon. For example, the Irish always seem to have the last word, they value storytelling, and although they may not agree with a person's opinion, they none the less will respect the person for having formed one, etc. The Greeks tend to value cooperation and support within the in-group but are defensive and hostile toward out-groups. Thus conversations are intense, incisive, combative, and loud. Cheating, and lying are acceptable when directed toward out-group members, etc.

The role play scenario is that these students are all members of a political science class. It is the beginning of the semester and the class syllabus indicates that there are roughly 100 articles to acquire and read for the semester. The class instructor has not placed these readings in any sort of package and therefore students are responsible for reproducing and reading the material themselves. The instructor indicated that the class should work together to organize, distribute, and finance the reproduction of the articles as a group and each student should come to class at the next class meeting two days later with all the articles. To make the interaction interesting and lively, the two groups of Greeks belong to different social clubs and the Irish students all live in the same neighborhood. Have the students role play the scenario using their assigned cultural communication characteristics and reach a plan to accomplish the assignment.

Test Items for Chapter 2

Multiple Choice

1. The primary difference between East Asian and North American perspectives on communication is that people of East Asian cultures such as the Chinese, Korean, and Japanese emphasize _____ more than North Americans.
   a. social relationships *
   b. individualism
   c. spirituality
   d. pragmatism

2. Which of the following most strongly forms the core of American culture and regulates interpersonal relationships in American society?
   a. freedom
   b. capitalism
   c. individualism *
   d. democracy

3. The cardinal Confucianism principle of *jen* most closely resembles which of the following practices?
   a. industriousness
   b. humility
   c. kindness
   d. reciprocity *

4. Which of the following is *not* among the five differences between East Asian and North American interpersonal relationship patterns?
   a. long-term versus short-term
   b. informal intermediaries versus contractual intermediaries
   c. negotiated versus conversational *
   d. particularistic versus universalistic

5. What kind of communication would most likely be used if one were concerned with face-saving during interpersonal communication?
   a. direct
   b. indirect *
   c. elaborated
   d. low-context

6. The use of "anticipatory communication" in Japan emphasizes the role of the _____ during interactions.
   a. relationship
   b. individual
   c. speaker
   d. listener *

7. Oral uncertainty reduction strategies are so necessary in U.S. society because
   a. of its diverse, heterogeneous population. *
   b. high-context messages are the norm.
   c. free speech is so highly prized.
   d. nonverbal communication is too ambiguous.

8. "Live and let live" is the essential spirit of which of the following religions?
   a. Hinduism *
   b. Islam
   c. Buddhism
   d. Sikhism

9. Action or activity is the definition of the Hindu term
   a. nirvana.   c. darma
   b. karma. *   d. Brahman

10. According to Hinduism, the ultimate aim in life is to
    a. help those who remain in the lower levels of existence.
    b. remain pure of heart and soul.
    c. realize the most profound level of existence. *
    d. experience interconnectedness among all other Hindus.

11. Which of the following statements would people who follow *karma yoga,* the third Hindu path to salvation, be most likely to say?
    a. Love lies at the base of every heart.
    b. Work can be a vehicle for self-transcendence. *
    c. Ignorance can be overcome through intense study.
    d. We must experience our bodies, our minds, and our spirits to their fullest potential.

12. What group of professionals is held in the highest esteem in Arab societies?
    a. bankers
    b. teachers
    c. businesspersons
    d. poets *

13. According to Anderson's article on Arab and American persuasive appeals, which of the following pairs of linguistic devices best characterizes Arab discourse?
    a. parallelism and overstatement *
    b. objectivity and directness
    c. soft tone and understatement
    d. syllogism and onomatopoeia

14. American discourse in newspapers is more likely than Arab discourse to include which of the following tactics to persuade an audience?
    a. parallelism
    b. emotional appeals
    c. linearity *
    d. rhythmic language

15. The organizing principle of the Saudi ad analyzed by Anderson was
    a. dialectic discourse.
    b. metaphoric association. *
    c. complicated abstraction.
    d. literal meaning.

16. Whereas Americans are more accustomed to explicitness in message design, Arabs make greater use of subtle cues during interaction. This dissimilarity is due to different processes of _____.
    a. contexting.
    b. verbalization.
    c. labeling. *
    d. nonverbalization.

17. Which of the following was the most important issue articulated in the Mobil (American) article?
    a. national honor
    b. justice
    c. peace
    d. economic necessities *

18. According to Triandis (In Broome's article) the Greek defines his world in terms of
    a. the intensity and satisfaction of interpersonal struggle and tension.
    b. a balance between the new and old.
    c. how many conflicts she/he can win.
    d. triumphs of the in-group over the out-group. *

19. What term (in English) is said to be the most cherished for Greek people?
    a. equality
    b. honor
    c. freedom *
    d. self-sufficiency

20. Which of the following is not associated with the Greek concept of *philotimo* regarding in-group behavior?
    a. obligation
    b. ethical morality *
    c. appropriate behavior
    d. self-esteem

21. According to Hirschon, what is the equivalent of "social death" to a Greek?
    a. withdrawal from others *
    b. loss of personal freedom
    c. damage to one's honor
    d. lack of personal space

22. What does *couvenda* refer to in Greek society?
    a. language
    b. communication
    c. conversation *
    d. conflict

23. Conflicts among members of Greek society usually tale place between
    a. males and females
    b. older and younger individuals
    c. members of different social groups
    d. in-groups and out-groups *

24. According to the value system of the Maasai:
    a. bodily adornment is important for adults but not children.
    b. young and old alike share equal status in society.
    c. the man with the most children is the wealthiest and happiest. *
    d. None of the above are true.

25. Which is not a component of the Maasai culture's worldview?
    a. the sacred cow *
    b. coexistence with nature
    c. religion
    d. death

26. What two primary language variables are used by the Maasai?
    a. sarcasm and singing
    b. stories and anecdotes
    c. directness and bluntness
    d. metaphors and proverbs *

27. In the Maasai culture, tough behavior might include which of the following?
    a. a great deal of opposite sex touching.
    b. the placing of the hands on children's heads as a sign of fondness. *
    c. very little same sex touching.
    d. children kissing elders.

28. Because of the brutal English rule, the Irish became an aural people so that:
    a. they did not have to write.
    b. the English could not decipher their language.
    c. they could have well versed lawyers to battle the English in court.
    d. they could preserve their cultural heritage. *

29. The intersection between the original Irish language, Irish Gaelic, and English has
    a.   made the Irish famous for their linguistic eloquence.
    b.   made them world renowned for their scintillating conversations.
    c.   given the Irish unparalleled success in language critical fields such as writing, law, and teaching.
    d.   all of the above. *

30. The talent for conversation is an art form that has not yet been lost in Ireland possibly due to:
    a.   the slow arrival of electronic technology and Irelands long suppression and isolation. *
    b.   the Irish wish to achieve fame from their storytelling.
    c.   the Irish combine conversation with visual art forms.
    d.   none of these answers are correct.

31. In Irish conversations:
    a.   children are excluded.
    b.   even the most mundane is expressed in a captivating manner. *
    c.   meaning is clear and direct.
    d.   It is considered rude for a young adult to converse with an elder in public.

True/False

T	1	Cultures of East Asia emphasize not an abstract concern for the general collective body but rather the maintenance of proper relationships among those bound by social networks.
F	2.	Confucianism is a highly mystical and metaphysical religion.
F	3.	Intermediaries in Korea tend to be people who help connect two individuals using formal, contractual processes.
T	4.	The English, Japanese, and Korean languages all employ codes to communicate status differences among listeners and speakers.
T	5.	In Japanese and Chinese communication, the responsibility of understanding what has been said is primarily the listener's.
F	6.	The deepest level of reality in the Hindu world view is understanding.
T	7.	The Hindu concept of *artha* refers to worldly success such as wealth, power, and fame.
F	8.	For Arab societies, the power of words lies in their ability to reflect human experience accurately.
F	9.	According to Anderson's analysis of Arab and American media, the Arab article wished to initiate purposefully a hostile reaction from American readers.
T	10.	Repetition and parallelism were linguistic devices used by the authors of the Arab editorial in the *Washington Post*.
T	11.	Each of the ads analyzed by Anderson assumed that the other nation's

view of the situation was similar to its own.

F   12. Conflict during an interaction always signals that something is wrong in the relationship.

F   13. It takes a great deal of time before a person will be accepted into an in-group of Greek society.

T   14. A strong sense of *philotimo* among Greeks can lead to intense conflicts without feelings of remorse or guilt.

T   15. Insults and attacks, within reason, are synonymous with conversing in Greek society.

F   16. According to Holden, relationships among Greeks tend to be quite stable and unchanging.

T   17. The history of the Maasai is the history of a people with an oral tradition.

F   18. The Maasai culture revolves around cattle and sheep.

T   19. The messages of the Maasai are full of elaborate symbolism.

F   20. Rather than being "past-oriented," the Maasai culture focuses on the present and the future.

T   21. In Ireland, "being" or the quality of life is valued more than "doing" or the pursuit of monetary gain.

T   22. Rather than give a simple verbal answer, the Irish tend to construct a vivid mental picture that is pleasing to both the mind and the ear.

T   23. Ireland has produced many prominent novelists, essayists, and poets reflecting the aural basis of the Irish.

T   24. One of the antecedents for the Irish love of conversation can be found in their intense curiosity.

Essay Questions

1. Describe the primary difference between East Asians and North Americans according to Yum's article.
2. Describe the four principles of Confucianism that form the basis of proper conduct.
3. Why wouldn't such North American practices as "Dutch treat" be seen favorably by Koreans?
4. Describe the four ways that Confucianism has had an impact on communication patterns among East Asian peoples.
5. Why are face-saving and "anticipatory communication" such important parts of East Asian communication?
6. What comprises the Hindu world view?
7. Describe the Hindu concepts of *karma* and reincarnation? How are they connected?
8. What do Hindus want most in life?
9. Describe the four different types of people that Hinduism recognizes.
10. What are the four Hindu paths to salvation?
11. Describe the different facets or types of *dharma* that guide a person through his or her life.
12. How does the caste system in India influence communication among its people?

13. Describe the linguistic devices used in both the Arab and American articles analyzed by Anderson. How are these culture-specific examples of discourse persuasive?
14. How did the process of "contexting" influence the use of discourse strategies in the Arab and American articles?
15. How are tension and struggle played in Greek geography, history, and interpersonal relations?
16. Describe how Greeks view in-groups and out-groups. How do these views influence communication and interpersonal relations with members of these groups?
17. What is *philotimo* and of what significance is it to Greeks and their interpersonal relations?
18. Using the information in Broome's article, describe a typical Greek conversation.
19. What functions does *couvenda* play in Greek society?
20. How are the phrases "the friend of my enemy is my enemy" and "what is past is forgotten" connected to Greek ways of communicating and relating?
21. How do different cultures conceptualize and practice such communicative experiences as interpersonal bonding, persuasion, and conflict?
22. What cultural patterns or beliefs of Hindus, Arabs, and Greeks most strongly influence these cultures' ways of communicating?
23. What problems might Arab and Hindu peoples have with Greek ways of communicating, especially ways of engaging in conflict? How might their styles correspond?
24. After reading the articles in Chapter 2, can you describe an Eastern way of communicating and a Western way of communicating?
25. What impact has history had on the Maasai culture?
26. Describe the three components of Maasai worldview and how these might impact communication.
27. Explain how Maasai proverbs are directly related to the Maasai value system.
28. Describe the verbal and nonverbal process typical of the Maasai during conversation.
29. Explain the importance of religion to the Irish and how this is manifested in conversation, in education, and in the family.
30. Identify specifics of beginning and ending a conversation as well as the strange turns the conversation may take among the Irish. Compare these to the typical North American conversation.
31. Gannon mentions several forums where conversation generally occur. identify them and their significance to the Irish worldview.

Chapter 3
Co-Cultures: Living in Two Cultures

Chapter Synopsis

This chapter examines the cultural patterns that influence the communication of certain cultural groups in the United States. Five distinct questions form the foundation of this chapter: (1) What does it mean and feel like to be the *other in* U.S. society? (2) How do power, dominance, and nondominance manifest themselves in intracultural U.S. communication? (3) What are some cultural characteristics of nondominant cultures in the U.S. and how do these differ from those of "mainstream" U.S. culture? (4) How do members of these cultures communicate intra- and interculturally? (5) With what challenges must members of these U.S. cultures contend as they live and communicate in the U.S.?

Edith Folb's article is an excellent discussion of how power and dominance are played out in U.S. society. Students will understand by reading Flob that U.S. society is dominated by the cultural institutions and artifacts of the power elite, institutions and artifacts to which members of nondominant cultures have little access. Ribeau, Baldwin, and Hecht's article will provide students with information about how African-Americans perceive their own and Euro-Americans' communication. Students will find this article especially useful in detailing specific cultural assumptions and expectations that African-Americans hold about communicating.

Wood focuses on the communicative patterns of women and men by delineating "masculine" and "feminine" culture. This article addresses the differences in the way women and men talk by referring to family relationships and children's games. This article will be most beneficial in helping students understand the influence that gender socialization has on how we communicate with members of the same and opposite sex. Braithwaite & Braithwaite and Majors' articles describe the experiences of members of two cultures who are often ignored and/or severely stigmatized within U.S. society. Braithwaite & Braithwaite use the comments of persons with disabilities to describe their experiences communicating with members of the "temporarily able-bodied" community. Students will receive valuable information not just about persons with disabilities but actually *from* persons with disabilities. The article's candor provides a source of rich discussion material. Finally, McKay illustrates through research literature and example, the characteristics of the co-culture of the elderly. This article will help students understand the complex and interesting lives that many elderly people lead. In addition, negative myths and stereotypes are dispelled and the special relationship between grandparents and grandchildren is explored.

Discussion Ideas

1. Ask students to engage in a class discussion on the following Orwellian quote: "All men are created equal--some are just more equal than others."

    a. Begin by inviting students to look closely at the terms in the sentence. Who is not included? What does "equal" mean? What does it mean to be "created equal"?

    b. Next, ask students to consider U.S. society. Who are the "some" that are more equal in the United States? Why are these people more equal than others? What do they have, what privileges do they have, that others don't? Who are those that are not "as equal" as those who are "more equal"? What prevents them from being as equal as the others? Use Folb's article to remind students of the historical construction of power, dominance, and nondominance in the U.S.

    c. Finally, ask students why, if we know that some people are more equal than others, does this situation persist in society today? Why hasn't it been changed? What will have to happen to make all people equal to each other? Is this possible? Are hierarchically structured, classist societies inevitable? Will there always be those on the bottom and those on top?

2. Do you think race relations can be improved between African-Americans and Euro-Americans using the several strategies provided by Ribeau, Baldwin, and Hecht for improving interethnic communication with African Americans? How could such strategies help? What else is necessary to improve U.S. race relations?

3. Why are nondisabled persons often so uncomfortable interacting with persons with disabilities?

    a. Ask students to consider this question by reflecting on their own experiences communicating with persons with disabilities. What made them uncomfortable? What was different about communicating with the person with a disability from communicating with nondisabled persons?

    b. Discuss the prevalence of uncertainty and unfamiliarity in intercultural communication. These feelings are very common and often account for much of our discomfort during intercultural interactions. What is often unfamiliar about communicating with persons with disabilities? What might we be uncertain about when we communicate with persons with disabilities?

    c. Using Braithwaite's suggestions as supporting material, ask students how they can go about becoming more comfortable with communication between themselves and persons with disabilities. What can they do? How can they view the other person?

4. How is gender a social phenomenon? Do you agree with Wood that our gender is the product of socialization? Or is it primarily, or at least partially, a biological phenomenon? Do you think male/female relations can be improved using the strategies that Wood suggests?

5. Prior to reading the McKay article, were you aware that many elderly people lead complex

and interesting lives? Do you know elderly people who do? Did you have or do you have a special relationship with a grandparent or both grandparents as described by McKay? Did/does this relationship help[you view other elderly people in a different light rather than via typical stereotypes?

Exercises

Exercise 3.1: Political Correctness or Necessary Changes? This exercise incorporates themes from all the articles in chapter 3. It asks students to consider the popular phrase "political correctness" and determine for themselves whether it is a movement that suppresses free speech or whether it is, in part, really about changes in our language and perception of other cultures. Changes in how we talk about and refer to people often lead to how we perceive those people. Take the evolution of the word *crippled* to refer to those individuals who use wheelchairs and walk with the aid of crutches. Over the past few decades, the word *crippled* went from *handicapped to disabled to physically challenged.* If you look at the progression of these terms and the more tolerant and inclusive social and legal changes that have affected physically challenged individuals, you can see a gradual positive development in how members of this group perceive themselves and are perceived by the able-bodied members of society. The same type of language evolution can be found in terms regarding African Americans, women, gays and lesbians, and the elderly. As our language changes, attitudes and policies sometimes change with it. Although there may not be a direct causal link between language changes and policy and attitude changes, it is clear that language can help us perceive the world and its people in different ways. With changes in perception come changes in how we act toward and interact with people. Guadalupe Friaz, assistant professor of ethnic studies at the University of Washington, describes language as political and always changing.

> When we talk about language we're talking about the relationships between people, and what people call each other reflects whatever tension and anxiety that society is going through.... Change is constant.... Group relationships always change, so of course terminology is going to change. (De Leon & Macdonald, 1992)

Change inevitably brings about many different kinds of tension and disagreement in a society. Decisions must be made about whether to make changes, how to go about making changes, who will make the changes, who will be affected, etc. Changes in our language, school curricula, and teaching strategies are just a few examples of the transitions taking place in the United States today as a result of a heightened awareness of diversity.

The term "political correctness" is often used to describe this increased awareness and shift toward more inclusive and specific language. Those who have coined the phrase "political correctness" feel that these changes in language and thought have bred a climate of intolerance on university campuses. Some people have perceived enormous pressure to use the *right* terms when talking about certain cultural groups. Others even feel that their freedom of speech has been suppressed when they are chastised for espousing views that are not in step with the current climate of multiculturalism and diversity.

Engage students in a dialogue about "political correctness" and what it means to them. We would suggest that you have students discuss several of the questions below in small groups and then have each group report out the results of their discussion. You may also wish to have students write on the general question of "What is political correctness?" the day before having a class discussion. This kind of exercise can turn into a very spirited and even emotional debate on the merits and disadvantages of "political correctness." Encourage students to be honest about their own opinions yet respectful of their classmates' opinions as well.

Some questions to consider in small groups and as a larger class:

1.   List some earlier terms used to identify African Americans, women, gays, lesbians, and the elderly. Then list the more recent politically correct terms.
2.   Define what you think the phrase "political correctness" means.
3.   Offer an alternative definition of "political -correctness," perhaps an opposing view from your own.
4.   Why have there been such negative opinions expressed in the media about political correctness? What's wrong with advocating and using "politically correct" language?
5.   What do you think about the linguistic and social changes that are currently taking place in our society?
6.   Do you feel that there is pressure to be "politically correct"? Or is being "politically correct" really just about being sensitive to and respectful of all members of U.S. society?
7.   What is there to be gained in our society by using language that refers more precisely to the cultural backgrounds of individuals? Conversely, what are the problems with using exact terms to refer to different groups of people?
8.   Consider this scenario. You are participating in a classroom discussion and use the word *black* to refer to U.S. citizens of African ancestry. A person in the class corrects you and explains that *African-American* is the preferred term. What is your reaction to this correction?
9.   How can we know how to refer to and address members of certain cultural groups?
10. Does it really matter what we call people? Can those people who are U.S. citizens just be called simply "Americans"? Why or why not?

Exercise 3.2: Privilege in U.S. Society. This exercise can be used with the Folb article. It asks students to examine U.S. society and determine which groups enjoy certain privileges to which many other groups do not have access. It is common among those who have the "room at the top" to assume that other individuals have equal access to society's opportunities, rights, and services, not realizing that people's personal worlds are made up of experiences that can be very culture-specific and biased against other groups. The assumption that people are the same and share the same societal benefits can strain and even hinder the development of intercultural relationships because such an assumption is based on a lack of awareness and sensitivity to an acquaintance, friend, or romantic partner's experiences. By examining the societal privileges that several groups enjoy, we can increase the awareness of and sensitivity to others' experiences that can be so crucial in intercultural communication.

One way to introduce this exercise on privilege in U.S. society to students is to begin with an example of Euro-American privilege. "White privilege" is a phrase used to identify advantages that many Euro-Americans have that are often not available to people of color. A serious and disturbing example of white privilege is the tendency for African-American men to be stopped for questioning by the police in upscale neighborhoods where they may be perceived as suspicious or "out of place." Euro-American males usually do not suffer this kind of discrimination under these same circumstances. While some groups may enjoy more privileges than others, all groups have greater access to certain privileges than others. For example, women, in general, are probably stopped by police for questioning less often than men. Thus we might say that white males more so than black males, and women more so than men, have greater access to the "privilege" of not being unnecessarily harassed by the police.

The questions below focus on issues of privilege and culture. Some will be very difficult for students because they will require information regarding cultural groups which they may know very little about. Most likely, the more diverse your class is, the more varied and informative will be the discussion. Ask students to consider many of the different cultural characteristics of U.S. society when answering the questions. For example, laws, societal norms, traditions, stereotypes, prejudices, etc. Students should first discuss these questions in small groups. Afterward engage the class in a discussion by having each group report on their responses. Watch for assumptions being made as the discussion progresses. That is, are statements being made that assume that students' experiences and perceptions are shared by other U.S. residents?

You may wish to give different questions to different groups so that all questions are covered. Add other questions not listed here and ask students to generate their own questions.

Questions

1. What societal privileges do you think Euro-Americans have greater access to than other cultural groups? Are there any privileges that non-Euro-Americans have that Euro-Americans do not?
2. What societal privileges do you think heterosexuals enjoy that gay men and women do not?
3. What societal privileges do men enjoy that women do not?
4. What societal privileges do women enjoy that men do not?
5. What societal privileges do able-bodied individuals enjoy that disabled individuals do not?
6. What societal privileges do same-race couples enjoy that different race couples do not?
7. What societal privileges do opposite-sex couples enjoy that same sex couples do not?

Exercise 3.3: Exploring Racial Relations. This exercise can be used with the Ribeau, Baldwin, & Hecht article. It asks students to reflect on communication effectiveness, communication issues, and communication improvement strategies identified in the article. Students are to examine a recent media issue involving Euro-Americans and African Americans. For example, the demonstrations and riots that took place after the "not guilty" verdicts were announced in the Rodney King police brutality trial, affirmative action issues, the O. J. Simpson trial, etc. Have the students analyze the effectiveness of the communication surrounding the event by determining if the seven primary issues of importance (negative stereotyping, acceptance, personal expressiveness, authenticity, understanding, goal attainment, and power dynamics) to African American were addressed/acknowledged/met, as well as issues of importance to Euro-Americans.

Other Questions to be Considered

Were any of the identified communication improvement strategies used? If so, what were they? How effective were they? If not, would the situation have improved if they were used?

How can both Euro-Americans and African Americans work together to improve their interaction?

Are these solutions possible on an institutional level as well as on a personal level?

What are some of your own solutions for improving interaction between Euro-Americans and African Americans?

Exercise 3.4: Interactions Among the Disabled and Able-Bodied. It is not uncommon for some people to feel uncomfortable around physically challenged individuals. Braithwaite & Braithwaite describes in their article the kind of communication that often occurs when an able-bodied and physically challenged person interact: greater physical distance, less eye contact, and shorter duration of talk. It is common for able-bodied, or "temporarily able-bodied," persons to focus on the disability instead of the person when interacting with disabled individuals. As a result, able-bodied individuals may be unsure of how to interact with less able-bodied people, and wonder nervously to themselves, "What can I say to this person *with a disability?*" They might do better to simply ask themselves, "What can I share with this person?"

Another feeling of uncertainty that might arise for an able-bodied person is how much assistance should they offer, or should they wait until a physically challenged person asks for assistance. When hearing people interact with members of the deaf culture, Jankowski (1991) says it is common for hearing people to believe that "they can explain things better because of the 'communication barrier' and will proceed with the conversation as though the deaf person were not there" (p. 149).

This exercise asks able-bodied students to consider their own feelings about and communicative behavior during interactions with disabled individuals. Ask students to read the following "Dear Abby" letter and answer the questions that follow in a small group. As with many of the exercises given in this manual, this exercise may be most effectively conducted by first having students consider in writing their perceptions of the disabled. Each group should have an opportunity to report their small group discussion findings in the larger class discussion.

Dear Abby:

> You have championed many causes for the physically challenged, and I thank you for all you have done. Now, will you please do us one more favor? Please advise waiters, waitresses, flight attendants, and everyone else who serves the public, of the following:

> Because a person happens to be in a wheelchair with leg braces--or appears to be partially paralyzed due to polio, cerebral palsy, a stroke or some unknown cause-- please do not assume that he of she can neither think nor speak. I was badly clobbered by polio many years ago, but have been rehabilitated greatly, thanks to physical therapy, my own determination and a lot of hard work. However, I am in a wheelchair and somewhat physically impaired. When I am in a restaurant (or on a plane) and food orders are being taken, please speak directly to me. Do not turn to my companion and ask, "And what will SHE have?"

CAN COMMUNICATE IN MARIETTA, OHIO

Some questions for discussion: Why do people often communicate with disabled persons in the manner described by "Can Communicate in Marietta"? What messages do they send to the disabled person when they communicate in this way? Have you ever felt uncomfortable communicating with someone who was in a wheelchair or in some way physically disabled or challenged? Why do you think you felt this way? What kept or keeps you from communicating, if at all, with a person who is disabled? Describe your last communication encounter with a disabled person. How can you break the communication barriers between you and a disabled person?

Exercise 3.5: Sexual Harassment or Friendly Behavior. Sexual harassment in professional environments has become a major and controversial issue in the past few years. It is an issue that has raised the consciousness of employers and employees, professors and students, and men and women in general. Sexual harassment is about many things: the abuse of power over subordinates and women, the definition of appropriate conduct in a working environment, and the right of all individuals to work in a nonthreatening, noncoercive setting. At a more basic level, however, sexual harassment is often about how the same behavior can be perceived quite differently by the people involved. This exercise focuses on male/female differences in behavior perception and can be used in conjunction with the Wood article.

This case study asks students to consider the role of perception in sexual harassment. Why do men and women often perceive the same behavior quite differently? How do men define "appropriate behavior" in the workplace? How do women define it? Before asking students to read and discuss the case study below in small groups, have them answer the first question about sexual harassment. Choose from among questions two through ten for students to answer with their group members; ask students to consider the remaining questions as a large class. Although this is a topic that lends itself to a great deal of debate and even conflict, encourage students to be as honest in their responses as possible.

Case Study on Sexual Harassment

1. How would you define sexual harassment? (Please don't give a legal definition. Draw from your own opinions and experiences.)

Susan worked as a welder for a small, privately owned auto parts manufacturer. After only a few weeks on the job, she began to notice that centerfold pin-ups from men's magazines were prominently displayed at individual work sites around the shop. There were also pictures of nude women tacked to the company's community bulletin board. Susan asked her only female colleague, Joan, why these pictures were there but Joan just shrugged her shoulders and said, "I guess because they like to look at them while they're working." Joan seemed unconcerned about the pictures.

But the pictures really bothered, even offended Susan. Susan felt that the pictures were pornographic and had no place in a work setting. She had to look at them whenever she went to talk to another employee or even pass their work stations, and she could not read the bulletin board without seeing the pictures there. After talking with her supervisor about her concern, he agreed to take down the pictures on the bulletin board but said that the men had a right to display the pictures at their individual work stations because that was their private space. Susan then asked individuals if they would display their centerfold pictures in less conspicuous places. All refused and said to "mellow out" because she was taking the issue too seriously. They felt the pictures were tasteful and anyway, "naked women are beautiful," they explained.

Susan was not convinced. She continued to ask her supervisor for help but, getting nowhere, went to the director of the company. He also did nothing. Meanwhile, it appeared that even more pictures were being put up in plain sight of Susan's work station. While a few men did understand her outrage, they did not join her in her struggle to eliminate the pictures. Frustrated with the situation, she quit her job after only six months.

2. Compare your definitions of sexual harassment. Are there differences among group members?
3. Based on your definitions, was Susan experiencing sexual harassment? Why or why not?
4. How did most of Susan's coworkers and her supervisor perceive the display of centerfold pictures?
5. Why was Susan reacting so strongly to these displays?

6. Whose perceptions of this situation do you support (if anyone's) in this case study? Explain your answer.
7. Do you feel that Susan's coworkers had a right to display pictures of nude women at their own work stations? Explain your answer.
8. What rights did Susan have as an employee of the company?
9. Given each of your answers above, how would you have resolved this controversy if you had been Susan? A fellow coworker? Her supervisor? Director of the company? Have one group member take on the role of one of these people and be prepared to report to the class their individual perspectives.
10. Do you think that women and men perceive sexual harassment differently? If so, how can such differences be resolved in the work place? Were there differences among your group members? If so, were these differences along gender lines?

Exercise 3.6: My Elder My Friend. This exercise is associated with the McKay article Understanding the Co-Culture of the Elderly and sends students into the "field" to actually experience this co-culture. The objective is to make the students aware of the complex and interesting lives led by many elderly and to encourage intergenerational relationships. Students may work alone or in groups on this assignment. They are to spend one hour with an *interesting* person whom they consider elderly. This person can be a relative, professor, acquaintance, etc. students should interview the person asking some of the following questions as well as any questions they would like to add. Students will then report their findings to the class.

Do you work or are you retired? Are you enjoying work/retirement?

What did you do that was particularly enjoyable this week?

Who are your closest friends? How often do you see them?

What are your hobbies?

Where did you go on your last trip?

Do you vote?

Do you have grandchildren? How often do you see them?

Do you feel that younger people don't understand you?

What things have you done in your life that you would change if you could?

What things have you done in your life that you are particularly proud of?

What is your favorite personal story?

What advice would you give to college students?

Test Items for Chapter 3

Multiple Choice

1. Intracultural communication broadly refers to communication that takes place within a
    a. heterogeneous environment.
    b. single, designated culture. *
    c. family unit.
    d. group of similarly minded people.

2. The presence of a power elite in a culture ensures what kind of relationship among the members of the society?
    a. symmetrical
    b. asymmetrical *
    c. relativistic
    d. linear

3. Which of the following words would best be used to characterize the notion of *a dominant culture* ?
    a. majority
    b. gender
    c. ethnicity
    d. power *

4. Who is Folb referring to when she speaks of individuals who bear a "visible caste mark" within U.S. society?
    a. the elderly
    b. ethnic minorities
    c. gays and lesbians
    d. all of the above *

5. What is one important aspect of any caste system?
    a. It is hereditary.
    b. One can rise to a higher level.
    c. You cannot progress to a higher level.
    d. It does not change.

6. Which of the following is NOT a stigmatized condition in the U.S.?
    a. female
    b. disabled
    c. elderly
    d. heterosexual *

7. Folb defines _____ as a set of behaviors.
   a. attitudes
   b. role *
   c. values
   d. communication

8. What kinds of characteristics most succinctly differentiate ethnic cultures from mainstream U.S. culture?
   a. linguistic and historical
   b. phenomenological and philosophical
   c. cognitive and material *
   d. economic and educational

9. In a study by Hecht and Ribeau (1984), Mexican Americans tended to view reward from a relationship in terms of
   a. whether a partner could provide something for them,
   b. the relationship itself. *
   c. how long they have known the person.
   d. family name and status.

10. Expressiveness, passion, and deep involvement with the topic are all ways that African-Americans demonstrate _____ in their communication.
    a. credibility
    b. friendliness
    c. righteousness
    d. genuineness *

11. The use of rigid racial categories that distort an African-American's individuality is called
    a. bigotry.
    b. negative stereotyping. *
    c. labeling.
    d. contexting.

12. What does "Mau Mauing" refer to in some African-American communication?
    a. being authentic
    b. joking around
    c. extreme assertiveness and confrontation *
    d. using subtlety and ambiguity

13. Taking turns and postponing discussing the problem until another conversation are both means of what kind of management?
    a. avoidance
    b. internal
    c. language
    d. interaction management *

14. How much of the population in some U.S. states is made up of disabled persons?
    a. 5 percent
    b. 7 percent *
    c. 10 percent
    d. 15 percent

15. Which of the following forms of redefinition by the disabled describes the following comment made by one of Braithwaite's informants: "I am a person like anyone else."
    a. redefinition as members of a new culture
    b. redefinition of self *
    c. redefinition of disability
    d. redefinition of life

16. Viewing a disability as a characteristic of a person rather than the person her or himself recognizes disability as
    a. inherent.
    b. inevitable.
    c. situational. *
    d. occupational.

17. The label "handicapped person" is problematic and objectionable to people with disabilities because it emphasizes the disability instead of the _____.
    a. culture.
    b. relationship.
    c. situation.
    d. person. *

18. Nonhandicapped or nondisabled persons are often referred to as _____ by members of the disabled culture.
    a. temporarily able-bodied *
    b. normal
    c. able-bodied
    d. futurely disabled

19. What is the cultural meaning of sex?
    a. sexuality
    b. gender *
    c. sexual orientation
    d. eroticism

20. A set of norms regarding how to communicate that is shared by a group of people is called a communication
    a. collective.
    b. community.
    c. culture.
    d. grouping.

21. What are the two primary influences on gender socialization?
    a. school and family
    b. media and school
    c. intimate and platonic relationships
    d. family dynamics and peer interaction *

22. When compared to boys' games, girls' games tend to include fewer people and rules are relatively
    a. ambiguous and unimportant.
    b. numerous and complex.
    c. set and rigid.
    d. unfixed and negotiated. *

23. Wood suggests that feedback and response cues such as "uh huh" and "hmm" from women can indicate which of the following to men?
    a. agreement *
    b. condescension
    c. desire
    d. weakness

24. Which of the following is NOT a severe consequence of stereotyping?
    a. The stereotyped group may engage in self-fulfilling behavior.
    b. Those who have preconceived notions may act upon their beliefs.
    c. The self-esteem and self confidence of the stereotyped group may suffer.
    d. Interactions may improve in a general sense. *

25. According to McKay, the "Golden Ager" is described as:
    a. active, adventurous, healthy, wealthy, and interesting. *
    b. retired, conservative, and old-fashioned.
    c. political and liberal.
    d. old and frumpy.

26. The elderly can be identified as co-culture because:
    a. They are distinguished from the larger culture. *
    b. They are a homogeneous group.
    c. They have many contributions to society.
    d. None of these answers are true.

27. One intergenerational relationship that seem to transcend the negative stereotypes of aging is:
    a. The relationship between parents and children.
    b. The relationship between grandparents and grandchildren. *
    c. The relationship of older siblings with younger siblings.
    d. All of the above.

28. McKay feels that there is as much diversity within the elderly population as between it and any other group because:
    a. the elderly have seen dramatic technological advances in their lifetime.
    b. they usually have had long-term marriages.
    c. they have lived through at least one war.
    d. all of the above. *

True/False

T	1.	Since 1965, the fastest growing population of people are those of non-European ancestry.
F	2.	A hierarchy of status and power does not exist in all cultures.
T	3.	Using force is not the most effective way to maintain one's position among the power elite.
T	4.	Those individuals who are most likely to hold and control positions of power in the U.S. are white, male, able-bodied, heterosexual, and youthful.
F	5.	Unlike India, the U.S. does not have a system where certain members of a society are born into a particular caste.
T	6.	The generating force behind power in the U.S. is economic.
F	7.	One study found that African-Americans tended to be more future oriented in their relationship development.
T	8.	One method of self-presentation among African-Americans is to deliberately contradict stereotypes.
F	9.	Acceptance, objectivity, and nondefensiveness are all forms of interaction management
T	10.	When stereotyping is taking place during a conversation, no communication strategies are seen as effective by African-Americans.
T	11.	Disability affects the behavioral, economic, and social aspects of a person's life.

F	12.	The nonverbal communication of an able-bodied person usually signals acceptance more so than the verbal message.
T	13.	No person is born with a particular gender.
T	14.	Girls and boys tend to define self in different ways.
T	15.	Senior citizens are as unique and diverse as most members of the younger population in our society.
F	16.	When using stereotypes as a form of categorization, individual differences are taken into account.
T	17.	Negative stereotypes of the elderly are created by young people, middle age people, and the elderly alike.
F	18.	Research indicates that intergenerational relationships rarely serve a productive function for either party.

Essay Questions

1. According to Folb, what is meant by the "dominant culture"?
2. Relate the following well-known quote to Folb's article: "All men are created equal--some are just more equal than others."
3. How are nondominant or "invisible" people in U.S. society often perceived by members of the dominant culture?
4. How are certain individuals in U.S. society stigmatized by the dominant culture? How are such slogans and phrases as "gay pride" and "Black is beautiful" a reaction to such stigmatization?
5. How does economics play a role in power and dominance in the U.S.?
6. What does the term *America* mean when used to refer to the U.S.?
7. How would you broadly define *appropriate and effective* communication? How can culture influence our perceptions of appropriate and effective communication?
8. How would you describe the communication of African-Americans and their expectations of conversational partners within their culture? How does this description compare to the communication of Euro-Americans and Mexican Americans?
9. Why did many of the African-American female respondents feel that toughness and "coolness" were important to convey during communication with whites? How and why does this communication differ from the need to be personally expressive and authentic in one's communication?
10. How are goal attainment and understanding connected in interethnic communication?
11. What are the two main themes of power dynamics in African-American speech?
12. Using the information provided by Ribeau, Baldwin, and Hecht, how can interethnic communication be improved?
13. What accounts for the rise in the number of persons with disabilities?
14. What's the difference between being disabled and handicapped?
15. What have been some problems with research on disabled persons' communication?
16. Describe the different ways that one becomes a member of the disabled culture?
17. What role does language play in the redefinition of disability for disabled and temporarily able-bodied persons?

18. What suggestions does Braithwaite give for communicating with people with disabilities?
19. How do sex and gender differ?
20. What is gender socialization?
21. How do the games of boys and girls differ and do such differences influence their communication patterns?
22. Using the examples provided by Wood, describe why men and women often have problems communicating?
23. How can men and women communicate more effectively?
24. Explain how interactions between young people and the elderly can result in lowered self-esteem and less self confidence for the elderly in future interactions.
25. Identify and describe the common communication thread among grandparent/grandchildren relationships that makes them so rewarding for both parties.
26. According to McKay, can we transcend the stereotypes of our aging population? If so How? If not, why not? What is your personal belief?
27. Using information from each of the articles in Chapter 3, how are nondominant U.S. cultures such as women, African-Americans, people with disabilities, gays and lesbians, and the elderly kept from obtaining equality, power, and respect by the "dominating culture"?
28. What do nondominant cultures such as women, African-Americans, people with disabilities, gays and lesbians, and the elderly have in common?
29. What must nondominant cultures do in order to survive and communicate within a society that is dominated by white, male, heterosexual, and able-bodied persons?
30. How is communication affected when people from the African-American and disabled communities perceive others as interacting with them using stereotypical views?
31. Taking the articles as a group, what suggestions can you give for communicating with members of nondominant U.S. cultures? Are there any suggestions that hold true for all of the cultures discussed in this chapter?

Chapter 4
Verbal Processes: Thinking and Speaking

Chapter Synopsis

The underlying premise of this chapter is that there is an important connection between culture and language. While some may argue that the primary linguistic difference between cultures is located in grammatical structures, the contention of this chapter is that language is much more than a set of words and phrases. The articles included in this chapter address the belief that in order to understand a culture, it is important to understand not only the grammatical structure of the primary language of the culture, but the ways in which members of that culture learn and actually use language on a day-to-day basis. Understanding language as it occurs in a particular situation provides a window through which a variety of aspects of culture can be viewed. The articles in this chapter will help readers understand that knowing how different cultures *use* language can be just as informative as knowledge of the native language itself.

Throughout this chapter students will be introduced to several variations on the theme of the interconnection between language and culture. In addition, they will have the opportunity to learn about a variety of forms of verbal communication that are found among and between cultures. After reading this chapter students should be able to articulate the perspective that members of a particular culture, as well as students exploring cultures, learn their culture through language.

Lieberman's article challenges students to make connections between thinking, problem solving, language, and culture. She argues that all are interconnected phenomena. her research compares and contrasts the problem-solving approaches encouraged by Japanese, Hebrew, French, Spanish, and English speaking teachers. Lee's article deals with a common problem faced by intercultural interactants -- the use of idioms. People from different cultures cannot assume that they understand each others use of idioms. Lee offers a processual method as a solution. Her method is based on the idea of explicit and elaborated communication that often characterizes low context cultures and is conducive to creating sharing and close relationships.

Carbaugh's article extends the relationship between language and culture by helping the students understand how a single language (English) can be used to express two different cultural meaning systems. He discusses Finnish and American rules for speaking in order to explain why many Finns find Americans superficial upon interaction with them. Orbe attempts to heighten the awareness of the issues surrounding African American male communication. He argues that there are six themes which represent the African American male strategy for coping with a European American male dominated society: the importance of other African Americans, learning how to communicate with non-African Americans, keeping a safe distance, playing the part, testing sincerity, and social responsibility.

Fong examines the role of language in human activity and its connection to culture. She overviews past, as well as current directions of culture and language research. She then draws from specific research on the Chinese culture to demonstrate the intersection of language and culture. Finally, Zormeier and Samovar introduce students to another language medium -- proverbs. Through an examination of Mexican-American proverbs students learn about Mexican-American cultural values.

Discussion Ideas

1.   What is meant by the statement that "language is a guide to social reality"?

2.   To what extent are the concepts of field dependence and independence, high and low context, and left and right hemisphere processing individual differences rather than cultural differences?
   a.   What difference would it make to the study of intercultural communication if these constructs were viewed as individual rather than cultural traits?
   b.   Would your concept of culture have to be expanded or limited with such a perspective?
   c.   Would you still be studying intercultural communication or would you be looking at interpersonal communication?

3.   Lee offers a processual solution to the problematic use of idioms. Is this a realistic solution? What alternatives might you think of?

4.   Carbaugh compares some of the conversational rules between Americans and Finns. Can you identify other American rules for conversation that he did not include in this essay?

5.   Orbe's co-researchers in no uncertain terms, indicated that they could never forget that "it's always whites ball." What does this mean? How is it manifested today? Is there any hope for optimistic future relations between African Americans and European Americans?

6.   Several researchers and scholars have abandoned the idea of linguistic relativity in order to focus on analysis of discourse. Do you feel that diversity in language categories and structure lead to cultural differences in thought and perceptions of the world? In what ways might linguistic relativity affect current analysis of discourse?

7.   Were Mexican-American values evident in the proverbs in the Zormeier and Samovar article? What other universal proverbs are you aware of? Name some proverbs that are specific to the United States or your native culture.

Exercises

Exercise 4.1 Language -- More Than Sounds. This activity can be used as an overarching exercise that links all the articles in the chapter. It asks students to explore the news media for examples of the various forms language can take in either an intracultural or intercultural interaction. From reading the chapter students have learned for example, that language involves sounds, meanings, forms of reasoning, techniques of problem solving, translation, linguistic devices such as analogies and idioms, ways of perceiving the world, specialized argot, and understanding sociocultural contexts. Have the students share their findings with the class.

Exercise 4.2. Eyes on Your Own Paper This exercise can be used in conjunction with Lieberman's article concerning culture, problem solving and pedagogical style. It points out numerous issues related to learning styles as well as testing and assessment across cultures. Have the students read the case study and answer the questions that follow.

Ulrike's parents sent her from Germany to school in the United States with the hope that she would improve her English language skills. Although she had studied English for many years in school and could speak it rather fluently, she did not have a good understanding of the more subtle aspects of the language. This was an area her parents wanted to see more fully developed.

Because of her apparent English language ability, the guidance counselor at her new school placed her with a full academic load. In one case in particular, her biology teacher, Ms. Reynolds, noticed that while taking tests Ulrike seemed to look at her neighbors paper from time to time. Ms. Reynolds tried to quietly warn Ulrike to keep her eyes on her own paper and that if she needed some help to simply ask and it would be provided. Ulrike, however, never asked for assistance and continued to glance at her neighbor's papers.

Finally, Ms. Reynolds had enough and confronted Ulrike with evidence that she had been cheating. Ulrike responded that she was aware that she looked at a few answers but insisted that she did not cheat on the whole test. She seemed to give the impression that she did not understand why the teacher would be so upset since there are so many tests that she would take. Ms. Reynolds is upset that Ulrike would cheat and feels that she is dishonest and too lazy to study hard (Cushner, 1994, pp. 112-113).

Discussion Questions

1. What insights could you provide to Ms. Reynolds that would help shed some light on the situation?
2. In what ways does culture influence the manner in which people problem solve and learn how to learn? How do these differences in learning styles affect educational gain?
3. What recovery skills might Ulrike employ to alleviate her current problem?

In this particular instance, Ulrike seems to be overwhelmed by the extreme number of tests that American students must complete. In Ulrike's native country, as in many places around the world, most of class time is spent studying, discussing, or otherwise "learning" the specific content of the course with little, if any, time devoted to testing. Testing is simply accomplished at the end of the term with students preparing for one major exam in the field of study to determine of she or he qualifies for the next level. Ulrike may find studying for tests on a weekly (or more) basis too demanding and distracting from the manner in which she is accustomed to learning. (Cushner, 1994, p. 121)

Exercise 4.3: Idiomatic Expressions. This activity can be used with Lee's article on idioms. This exercise demonstrates the difficulty in explaining and translating idioms to people who do not come from the same culture. Students will learn that idioms are very culture-bound and that knowing a language such as English does not ensure that one will understand all the idioms of the English language. This activity can be carried out in several ways. One way is to ask students to generate their own list of idioms and explain their definitions. Divide the class into groups of four to six students. Ask them to generate as many English idioms as they can think of from the U.S. This may be difficult at first because idioms are such a natural, unconscious part of conversation so it might be wise to give a few examples to get students started. Then ask each group to explain each idiom using Lee's processual method for idioms and intercultural communication competence. Having international students in your classroom will enhance this exercise because many of them may not be familiar with all U.S. idioms. Students will discover that many idioms are difficult to define because native speakers of any language know the idioms of their culture intuitively through years of usage. Discuss the possible origins for the idioms that students generate.

A second way to carry out this activity is to use the handout that follows entitled "Idiomatic Expressions in English" that lists English idioms from three different cultures: the United States, Great Britain, and the Bahamas. Ask students to first explain what the U.S. idioms mean. Again, international students may act as "judges" who determine whether the explanation of an idiom is adequate and whether understanding has been achieved. Then ask students to try to define the idioms in the other two lists. Which do they know, which can they accurately guess the meanings of, and which do they not understand? Give them the definitions to the British and Bahamian idioms and discuss possible reasons why these idioms were constructed the way they were.

Possible questions for discussion: Why is it difficult to explain idioms from our own culture? Did Lee's Processual method help? How do you think idioms are formed? Why do they cause a great deal of trouble for normative speakers of any language? Can you think of any idioms from the U.S. that you used to not understand but now do? Could these idioms have been regionally based? How did you come to understand each of these idioms? Did you ask for an explanation, or was the meaning clear contextually?

Exercise 4.3: Idiomatic Expressions in English: Cultural Differences

UNITED STATES

bite the dust
blow off steam
bone to pick
blow the whistle on
bored to tears
bread and butter
break the ice
brush off
beat around the bush
change one's tune
chip on one's shoulder
climb on the bandwagon

face the music
fair-weather friend
fed up
fine-tooth comb
get one's feet wet
get through one's head
feet on the ground
give up the ship
go against the grain
go to pot
in the family way
in the long run

keep your shirt on
land on one's feet
make no bones
neither here nor there
on the fence
on the whole
pay the piper
read between the lines
scratch the surface
save one's breath
miss the boat
take a back seat

GREAT BRITAIN

applaud to the echo
in bad odour
to be on (off) the beam
chop and change
as cold as charity
have a crow to pluck (pick)
die in harness
dree one's weird
hang on a person's lips
come to heel

feel like a giant refreshed
of the first water
go to one's account
not as green as he's cabbage
    looking
help a lame dog over a stile
a pretty pass
improve the occasion
have one's knife in a person
late in the field

lose caste
lose the day
merry as a cricket
with might and main
grasp the nettle
put in one's oar
shilly-shally
from pillar to post
pink of perfection
to stump up

THE BAHAMAS

bitch up
broad-speaking
get burned up
butter for fat
that's chalk
cheek somebody up
clap somebody up
cold in the arm, leg
curry-favor someone
cut up with someone
cut your grass
decide your mind

what the diggins
dive up
doggy after someone
don't-care-'f-I
draw hand
eat off someone
fowled of doing something
pick up gap seed
grind somebody up in your
    heart
in quest
keep somebody hot

land somebody off
lay on your chest/stomach
make him know
make your break
mix fool with sense
one mind tell me
own something to somebody
pick somebody's mouth
pick up for somebody
pitch a stink
poke death with a stick
rap someone up

Exercise 4.3: Idiomatic Expressions in English

Key

<u>GREAT BRITAIN</u>
(Collins, 1958) Note: some of these may no longer be used in everyday conversation.

applaud to the echo: to acclaim and clap loudly, so that one rouses echoes.

in bad odour: in disfavour, in disrepute.

to be on/off the beam: to be on or off the point, to be relevant or irrelevant.

chop and change: to be constantly changing, generally used derogatorily.

as cold as charity: lacking in signs of warm emotion.

have a crow to pluck (pick): to have a complaint or criticism to make.

die in harness: to die while still actively engaged in the course of one's regular work.

dree one's weird: to endure with philosophic resignation what happens to one ("dree" "weird" -- fate).

hang on a person's lips: to listen closely to; similar to *hang on a person's every word*

come to heel: to show humble and complete obedience.

feel like a giant refreshed: to feel physically or morally strong after something has happened.

of the first water: of the most excellent kind.

go to one's account: to die.

not as green as he's cabbage-looking: not so simple as one might think: not such a fool as he looks.

help a lame dog over a stile: help a person deal with a difficulty with which he/she is incapable of coping.

a pretty pass: a serious state of affairs.

improve the occasion: to seize every advantage one can out of the circumstance.

have one's knife in a person: to be constantly finding occasions for complaining about or blaming a person.

late in the field: late on the scene.

lose caste: to forfeit one social position by doing something that is regarded as socially discreditable.

lose the day: to be defeated.

merry as a cricket: extremely cheerful.

with might and main: with all one's power.

grasp the nettle: to tackle a difficulty or danger boldly.

put in one's oar: to intervene in action or discussion.

shilly-shally: to vacillate, waver, be undecided, hesitate.

from pillar to post: to move from one place or resource to another.

pink of perfection: the highest degree of what is perfect of its kind.

to stump up: to pay money.

Exercise 4.3: Idiomatic Expressions in English

Key

<u>THE BAHAMAS</u>   (Holm, 1982)

bitch up: to ruin, spoil; to frustrate.

broad-speaking: plain-speaking, outspoken.

get burned up: to become exhausted through physical exertion.

butter for fat: like for like; similar to *tit for tat*.

that's chalk: that's inevitable; a foregone conclusion; slang for *that's great*.

cheek somebody up: to be impertinent to somebody.

clap somebody up: to applaud somebody; similar to *applaud to the echo*.

cold in the arm, leg: an inflammation of the arm or leg.

curry-favor someone: give somebody an unfair advantage because of personal connections; curry somebody's favor.

cut-up with someone: to flirt.

cut your grass: to usurp someone else's prerogative or exclusive right or privilege.

decide your mind. to make a decision.

what the diggins: an exclamation of surprise.

dive up: to dive into the water and bring something up.

doggy after someone: to follow someone about constantly.

don't-care-f-1: not caring, especially about social norms.

draw hand.- to make a leading or beckoning gesture.

eat off someone: to eat at someone else's expense.

fowled of doing something: engaged in doing something.

pick up gap seed: to gather information for gossip.

grind somebody up in your heart: to bear a grudge against somebody.

in quest: to admit defeat in playing cards or marbles.

keep somebody hot. to be at a person's heals, getting in his/her way.

land somebody off. to drop someone off from a car or boat.

lay on your chest/stomach: to cause indigestion or nightmares (of food eaten late at night).

make him know: to scold or punish.

make your break: to seize an opportunity to do what one has been wanting to do.

mix fool with sense: to attempt to deceive someone by interspersing lies with the truth.

one mind tell me: I had a vague contradictory feeling (that something would happen, etc.).

own something to somebody: to confess something to somebody.

pick somebody's mouth: to get information by engaging in seemingly casual conversation.

pick up for somebody: to take somebody's side of the argument.

pitch a stink: to object vehemently, cause a commotion.

poke Death with a stick: to court danger, to tempt fate.

rap someone up: to applaud someone, especially for a generous donation to a church.

Exercise 4.4 Same Native Language Students have learned from Carbaugh's article on Finnish and American cultures linguistic action that sharing the same native language does not necessarily mean smooth interaction. This case study will further amplify the notion that sharing a common language does not necessarily mean there will be few, if any adjustment difficulties.

On the outside, speakers of the same language may appear to communicate and understand one another. Critical problems often present themselves as individuals may delve into rather sensitive issues, oftentimes unknowingly, long before any real sense of trust and understanding has been developed. This is especially evident when students form the United States take their rather forthright and apparently open attitude with them to another English-speaking country. (Cushner, 1994, p. 97)

Have the students read the following case study and answer the questions that follow.

John had left his home in Wisconsin only 36 hours earlier and found it quite amazing that he was now in New Zealand along with 75 other students who came from 14 countries. He, as well as these other students, were about to embark on the experience of a lifetime -- that of spending 1 year living with a new family and attending school in New Zealand. As was customary, new arrivals into New Zealand would spend about 2 days at a brief "Gateway Orientation," sleeping off their jet lag and being introduced to essentials of life in their new home. All along, John was certain he would have a relatively easy time adjusting to his new country. This sense was reinforced during the Gateway Orientation when he observed students from such places as Japan, Thailand, and France struggling with their English. Why, John's native language was the same as those in New Zealand, so what could possibly go wrong? He left the Gateway Orientation rested and eager to merge with his family and new school. He confidently said good-bye to the orientation staff, expecting to see them a few weeks later at another gathering.

At the next gathering of students and staff from around the country, John was singled out by local volunteers as having quite severe adjustment problems. His host parents thought him abrasive, and his host brothers and sister complained that he was nosy and too inquisitive. john complained that people were too literal, maintained only "surface-level" relationships, and did not appear to be sincerely interested in developing close interpersonal relationships (Cushner, 1994, p. 93-94).

Discussion Questions

1. If you were a counselor for the exchange organization, where might you focus your discussion with John?
2. What is the connection between language and culture in this situation?
3. What might John do to improve this situation?

Exercise 4.5: Language and Shared Experience. This exercise can be used with Orbe's article studying African American male communication. Orbe identifies the notion of "playing the part" as an African American strategy to cope while communicating with European Americans. This exercise asks students to think about the many ways they "play the part" when they interact with different people in their lives. Do they discuss different topics, use different words, and have a different way of reacting to these various groups of people? Our language changes as the people with whom we converse change. To talk with everyone in the same way would mean we have the same kinds of relationships with all the people in our lives. This, of course, is not the case.

This exercise explores the culture-specific use of language among certain groups of people. It asks students to consider how they talk with different groups of people in their lives and how they feel about such culturally specific and possibly restricted communication. This activity can be done in small groups, as a large class discussion, or a combination of both.

Different Language Styles

1. Compare the way you talk with different groups of people in your life (see below). Consider differences regarding what you talk about, your responses, and your feelings while communicating.

    a. parents vs. friends
    b. brothers vs. sisters
    c. teachers vs. friends
    d. spouse/girlfriend/boyfriend vs. friends
    e. supervisor vs. coworker
    f. men vs. women
    g. members of your culture vs. other cultural members
    h. other groups

2. Why does your language change depending on which group of individuals you are interacting with?
3. How does shared experience influence how you interact with people?
4. Do power and role influence your interactions?
5. Do you think it is fine for members of one culture to use language with each other in ways that would be considered offensive or inappropriate for other cultural groups? Why or why not?
6. Do you talk with men and women differently? Why or why not? If yes, provide some examples.
7. Have you ever used language that a person from another cultural group found offensive? If yes, describe the situation.

Exercise 4.6: Words Are Outside, Meanings Are Inside. This activity can be used with Fong's article exploring different perceptions on the connection between language and culture. Because people come to an interaction with different perceptions about the world, they will not understand exactly the same thing when they hear or use a word. Even among culturally similar individuals, perceptions will differ and the meanings we ascribe to the words we use will not always be shared by those who are like us. The maxim "meanings are in people" refers to the notion that words do not hold meaning, people hold meaning. Words allow us to get our meanings across to others but they do not by themselves constitute meaning. We give words meaning based on our experiences, experiences that are often culture-specific. This exercise helps demonstrate the interconnection of language, meaning, experience, and culture.

This exercise asks students to reflect on what meanings they hold of certain words and how those meanings might differ from those held by people of other cultural groups. Ask students to characterize what they think the following words mean to them by using each in a complete, "illustrative" sentence: preacher, atheist, feminist, communism, Texan, capitalism, liberal, lesbian, sexist, and bigot. Add words that you feel would be especially suited for this exercise. By "illustrative" we mean a definition that illustrates or characterizes *to students* what these labels or concepts mean. For example, for the word *teenager* someone might write: "Someone who doesn't listen to their parents, doesn't trust anyone over thirty, and believes they are invincible." After students write a sentence for each word, ask them to share their responses with a group of their classmates.

Some questions to ask students during their small group or a class discussion: How did you arrive at your own meaning of each of the words? What differences and similarities were there among the sentences? What might account for such differences and similarities? Do you think your definitions are shared by most or few people in the U.S.? Who do you think would share your definitions? Have you ever had a conversation with someone from your own culture or another culture who had a very different meaning for a word than your own definition? How might the differences we ascribe to certain words and concepts affect our interactions with people who do not share our cultural background?

Exercise 4.7: Proverbs. This activity is designed to be used in conjunction with the Zormeier and Samovar article on Mexican-American proverbs. It is said in Burundi that "Proverbs are the daughters of experience." Proverbs are one way that a culture teaches its members appropriate conduct, including effective ways of communication. Consider this cultural proverb well known to people in the United States: 'You scratch my back, I'll scratch yours." This saying alludes to a rule of negotiation based on compromise and give and take. The Zairean proverb, "A little subtleness is better than a lot of force" suggests to members of this African culture that one should not be too pushy and overbearing when communicating. Proverbs are one way that our culture passes on wisdom. Zormeier and Samovar discuss proverbs that are universal and proverbs that are specific. Have the students share some specific proverbs that their families have taught them. For example, many Jewish children hear the proverb that "With money in your pocket, you are wise and you are handsome and you sing well too." Have students identify how these familial proverbs have impacted their lives. Be aware of any contrasting proverbs among the students. For example, "Honesty is the best policy" versus "Little white lies never hurt anyone." Contrasting proverbs can lead to a lively discussion when their implications are analyzed by the class.

Test Items For Chapter 4

Multiple Choice

1. Connotative meanings are those that
   a. indicate a specific "thing" to which a symbol refers.
   b. indicate an evaluative dimension. *
   c. have a physical correspondence.
   d. are always considered to be positive.

2. Which of the following is NOT a major theme in Lieberman's article on problem solving?
   a. possible reasons for cultural differences in problem-solving processes
   b. teaching styles reinforce culture-specific styles of solving problems
   c. U.S. problem solving processes are universally understood *
   d. problem solving processes are grounded in culture

3. Which of the following terms is NOT associated with right-hemisphere problem solving?
   a. nonverbal communication
   b. holistic thinking
   c. intuition
   d. cause-effect *

4. Field independent individuals typically
   a. perceive events holistically.
   b. organize details in linear, cause-effect sequences. *
   c. register emotions and feelings with events.
   d. enjoy working with others to solve problems.

5. Cultures in which members exhibit a tendency toward collectivism are also likely to be
   a. high-context cultures. *
   b. intolerant of ambiguity.
   c. field independent.
   d. analytic problem solvers.

6. In Lieberman's study, which of the following verbal differences was NOT noted between the cultures?
   a. intolerance of ambiguity
   b. individualistic vs. collective reasoning
   c. encouragement of reflectivity
   d. student/teacher touching behaviors *

7. A complete explanation of an idiom involves:
   a. a linguistic discussion of the meaning of words.
   b. a relational discussion about the relationship of the two people using the idiom.
   c. a linguistic an a relational discussion. *
   d. None of the above.

8. If people from different cultural backgrounds can use each others idioms, intercultural relationships may be facilitated because:
   a. a sense of informality an closeness will be established. *
   b. formality will be established.
   c. casual acquaintances will increase.
   d. None of the above.

9. A primary difference between goal-oriented talk and metatalk is:
   a. metatalk is superficial.
   b. goal-oriented talk assumes a shared lifeworld. *
   c. in goal-oriented talk people understand each other completely.
   d. metatalk involves a third person.

10. Transforming single descriptive talk into double/multiple descriptive talk involves:
    a. reconstructing alternatives. *
    b. focusing on essential thinking.
    c. an examination of linguistic metatalk.
    d. None of the above.

11. Americans may appear superficial to Finns because
    a. Americans often say more than the social situation warrants.
    b. Finns think the use of superlatives like "absolutely gorgeous" are presumptuous and immodest.
    c. Americans state the obvious.
    d. All of the above. *

12. Americans tend to use small talk because
    a. it forms a civil link between diverse people. *
    b. they do not value self disclosure.
    c. they feel constraints should be placed on what is discussed.
    d. None of the above.

13. According to communication patterns of Finns, if one engages in conversation with another for a period of time
    a. the individuals have "bonded."
    b. both people have left an impression.
    c. both people are obligated to subsequent interaction. *
    d. None of the above.

14. For the African American male, intra-ethnic communication serves as
    a. a surface tension release.
    b. obligated conversation.
    c. a barrier device.
    d. a measurement of one's success. *

15. Most of the African American males in Orbe's study attributed their learning to interact with non-African Americans to
    a. direct talks with others.
    b. observations.
    c. trial and error.
    d. all of the above. *

16. European Americans were perceived as allies by the African American males in Orbe's study if they
    a. always tried to be politically correct.
    b. invited African Americans to their house.
    c. said some of their best friends were black.
    d. came across as sensitive, sincere, honest, an open. *

17. In the first half of this century, scholars examined language itself as an object of study, but the second half of the century focused on
    a. grammar and syntax.
    b. analysis of languages function in a sociocultural context. *
    c. structural rules.
    d. language autonomy.

18. Qualitative research methods examine the interrelationship of language and culture through
    a. ethnography.
    b. pragmatics.
    c. discourse analysis.
    d. all of the above. *

19. The unfortunate incident of breaking a glass object during Chinese New Year is transformed to a fortunate incident when
    a. the object is replaced.
    b. the person breaking the object says a prayer.
    c. the person orally uses a positive expression to describe the unfortunate act. *
    d. by redescribing the incident as a purposeful gesture.

20. Proverbs have an impact on human behavior because
    a. they teach children what to expect from life.
    b. they capture what a culture deems important.
    c. they are handed down form one generation to the next.
    d. all of the above. *

21. The two categories of proverbs identified by Zormeier and Samovar are
    a. advice-giving and scolding
    b. universal and specific *
    c. condensed and elongated
    d. traditional and modern

22. In the Mexican-American culture proverbs are repeated most often by
    a. women scolding children
    b. fathers giving advice
    c. singers
    d. all of the above *

23. "He who is born to be a potted plant will never go beyond the porch" can be interpreted to mean
    a. stay close to your family.
    b. honor and integrity are found in the home.
    c. support your family before helping others.
    d. each person has a certain place in life which cannot be changed. *

True/False

T   1   Cultures that tend to encourage and reward individuals who display field independence also tend to reward impulsivity and intolerance of ambiguity.

F   2.   According to Lieberman's article, it is not necessary to learn the logic and problem-solving approaches encouraged in a culture to learn the language of that culture.

T   3.   In the United States, the primary form of problem solving advocated in the educational system is consistent with traditionally accepted left hemisphere problem-solving skills.

F   4.   An idiom and its meaning often do not match because they have literal rather than figurative relationship.

T   5.   The first step in Wen Shu Lee's creative process involves working together to establish a conversation in which it is acceptable to bring up problems.

T   6.   Double descriptive talk requires an identification of two things that differ.

T   7.   Americans distinguish between "friendliness" and "friendship."

F   8.   There may be significant periods of silence in Finnish conversations because their culture places a low value on talk.

T   9.   Finns feel obligated to make their talk nonobvious, socially worthwhile, and non-contentious.

T   10.   The African American men involved in Orbe's study felt that other African Americans were better able to understand their problems.

F   11.   For the African American male, communication with European American males serves as a form of motivation.

T	12.	"Playing the part" involves abandoning the communication styles of the African community and adopting those associated with the dominant European American culture.
F	13.	"Playing the part" and "keeping a safe distance" from European Americans are safe, effective, no risk strategies for African Americans.
T	14.	According to the Sapir-Whorf hypothesis, language influences and shapes how people perceive their world and their culture.
F	15.	In general, the Sapir-Whorf hypothesis has come to be regarded as confirmable and correct.
F	16.	Chinese immigrants value immodesty and have little problem accepting direct compliments from Americans.
T	17.	By discovering the meaning of a proverb one can understand something of what is important to its user.
T	18.	In nearly every culture there is a proverb stressing hard work.
F	19.	The proverb "Give time to time" reflects the strong past orientation of Mexican-Americans.
F	20.	Proverbs are unique because they contain detailed pieces of wisdom that can be easily used by anyone in that culture.

Essay Questions

1. Differentiate between *field dependent and field independent* cognitive styles.
2. Lieberman stresses the importance of viewing cultural differences along a continuum rather than through an either-or perspective. Explain her perspective with regard to BOTH the distinction between high- and low-context cultures and individualism and collectivism.
3. In your own words, define the "cultural cognition" paradox.
4. Identify and explain the four steps in Wen Shu Lee's processual method for overcoming idiom misunderstandings.
5. Explain what low-context communication has to do with Wen Shu Lee's processual method for overcoming idiom misunderstandings.
6. Identify and explain the primary ways that Finns and Americans differ in their linguistic use.
7. Explain what Carbaugh means when he says, "the crucial variable when treating culture and communication is not fundamentally the language that is used, but the patterned ways in which the language is used, and the cultural meanings associated with them." Give examples.
8. Describe the dilemma faced by African American males when "playing the part" and "keeping a safe distance from European American males."
9. Why did the African American males in Orbe's study feel an intense social responsibility to assist other African American males?
10. Explain how Fong's cultural case study of the Chinese use of language to reverse bad luck reflects new trends in language and cultural research.
11. To what is Fong referring in the title of the article "The Crossroads of Language and Culture?"
12. Based on the readings in this chapter, articulate the relationship between language and culture. Include examples and supporting material from at least three different articles.

13. One of the primary assertions of this chapter has been that there is more to language than grammar. Using information in the articles by Carbaugh and Orbe, explain your understanding of this assertion.

14. If you were a corporate trainer for a multinational corporation that does business in countries around the world, what specific information about language would you include in a training program for your international sales personnel to help them be more effective in their intercultural interactions?

15. Explain the notion that many of the same proverbs can be found in nearly all cultures.

16. Explain the Mexican-American proverb "Better to be a fool with the crowd than wise by oneself" in terms of the Mexican-American value it exemplifies.

17. Explain the message communicated in the following Mexican-American proverb, "We are like well buckets, one goes up and the other comes down."

18. What are some of the most important values for the Mexican-American culture and how are these values communicated through proverbs?

Chapter 5
Nonverbal Interaction: Action, Sound, and Silence

Chapter Synopsis

The major premise of this chapter is that successful intercultural communication requires more than an understanding of verbal interaction. Nonverbal behavior also provides important insight into cultural patterns of communication. In this chapter students will be introduced to the role and impact of movement, personal space, touch, time, gender, paralanguage and silence in a variety of cultural contexts. As the editors note, nonverbal communication often serves as the frame for interpreting verbal communication, so learning about some of the patterns of communicating without words offers students of intercultural communication a broader understanding of communication among and between cultures.

The assumption that nonverbal behaviors are for the most part unconscious behaviors undergirds this chapter. It is important for students to note that any portrayal of the nonverbal behaviors described as typical from one culture to the next are not characterizations of behaviors that are formally "taught" within each culture. Students who wish to communicate more effectively interculturally should not expect to "learn" appropriate nonverbal behaviors simply by reading about them in the text. Rather, what this text offers is a way of viewing behaviors that students might otherwise misinterpret for noncommunicative events.

Andersen's article provides a thorough overview of nonverbal communication and its relationship to culture. In fact, he argues that culture is primarily a nonverbal phenomena. McDaniel uses the Japanese as a cultural model to illustrate how nonverbal communication practices function as a reflection, or representation of societal cultural themes. Students will learn how cultural influences can subtlety shape a society's nonverbal communication behavior. Emphasizing another nonverbal communication- feature, Dolphin explores the use of space in human interaction. Similarities and differences in the use of personal space are discussed with respect to cultural variation. Finally, Hall provides an interesting description of time as a nonverbal feature of communication. Again, students may find themselves wondering about the ways in which time is a communicative variable among cultures. Hall's distinction between monochromic and polychronic time introduces students to some of the interaction forms that may emerge as a result of cultural differences regarding time.

Discussion Ideas

1. According to Andersen, "culture is primarily a nonverbal phenomenon." To what extent do you agree or disagree with his conclusion?

   a. If we are to accept his claim that culture is not learned through explicit verbal instruction, what value is there in training people to be more interculturally aware?

b.   Encourage students to think about their own experiences with other cultures. If they say that they have never had any experience with a culture other than their own, suggest that they think about organizations, classrooms, and families as cultures. How have they learned how to behave appropriately in new cultures? Via explicit verbal instruction or by watching and learning through repeated observation of what people do?

2.   What does it mean to say that one culture is more masculine than another? What is the relationship between the communication that occurs in cultures labeled as masculine and the role of women within the culture? The role of men?

3.   Many people assume that we can learn to read a person's nonverbal communication like a book. There are even popular press books published on the subject. Andersen argues that we cannot read members of our own cultures let alone members of another culture. To what extent do you agree or disagree with his conclusion?

4.   How might the homogeneity of the Japanese affect consistent themes in society? Compare the Japanese situation to that in the U.S.?

5.   What problems would you anticipate between dating partners, one of whom comes from a high-context culture and the other from a low context culture?

6.   What differences can you identify from your own experience regarding the distance at which you communicate with men and women? What do you believe accounts for those differences?

7.   Of what benefit is learning about cultural differences and similarities with regard to personal distance? What impact might there be if you were to ignore cultural norms for personal space when communicating with others?

8.   Hall differentiates between monochromic and polychronic time, indicating that different cultures operate with different perspectives of time. Do you feel that these orientations to time are limited to cultural distinctions or do individuals operate on different times as well? What are some of the potential ramifications for business and personal interactions when parties to the communicative event have different perceptions of time?

9.   How are nonverbal factors of communication between and among cultures related to the verbal components of language discussed in the previous chapter?

10.   Given the complexity of language, what advice would you have for someone who hopes to not only understand, but take part in the day-to-day life of another culture?

Exercises

Exercise 5.1: Nonverbal Greeting/Leave-Taking Behaviors. This activity is designed to incorporate all the articles in chapter 5 by heightening the students' awareness of how they take part in greeting and leave-taking behaviors and how these behaviors might be vastly different from other cultures of the world. This exercise will also make students aware of their own level of comfort in touching and being touched as well as their preferred space distance. Begin by dividing the class into two subgroups, X and Y, which represent groups of business professionals from two different cultures. Distinguish the two groups with something obvious such as colorful armbands, name tags, or ribbons. Ask Team Y to leave the room. You may give the teams written or verbal instructions.

Instruct Team X members that when Team Y comes back into the room they are to meet and greet their friends and business associates who are Team Y members. Inform Team X members that they come from a culture where close contact and warm embraces are the traditional style of saying "hello." Point out that when they shake hands on encountering Team Y members they must prolong the handshake for a least thirty seconds. Then they should make small talk for a few minutes (ask about family members, school, sports etc. but do not engage in discussions of business, instead, redirect the conversation to other non-business topics), standing a little closer than is normally comfortable for them. A bell should ring after a few minutes and then Team X should say good-bye by giving their partner a warm embrace.

Instruct Team Y members that when they reenter the room they are to meet and greet members of Team X as friends and business associates in the traditional fashion of U.S. organizational culture by shaking hands. Team Y's objective is to begin a business transaction with Team X. They should say good-bye when the bell rings by shaking hands. The entire interaction should last for no more than three to four minutes.

Facilitate a debriefing session by asking for student comments about how they felt during the exercise. Discuss the awkwardness evident when different nonverbal rules were being used during the interaction. If you have a culturally diverse classroom, you will obviously get very different responses. These responses will undoubtedly enrich the discussion by lending first-hand insight into the touch and proxemic behavior of various cultural groups. Discuss with students the extent to which members of U.S. cultures engage in public touch behavior, when, and with whom. Also, talk with students about other cultures around the globe that engage in same-sex touching in public. For example, in Kenya and Nigeria men walk hand-in-hand frequently yet mixed-sex hand holding is rarely seen. In some African countries, handshakes are often extended, not quick, firm grasps as is often the case in the U.S. Ask team Y if they felt frustrated at team X's refusal to talk about business. While U.S. business people are often in a "hurry" to get down to business, other cultures prefer to establish friendships before conducting business. This represents a different time orientation than is typical in the U.S.

Possible questions for further discussion: What happens when someone touches more than we are used to? How do we respond? Why? When do you feel comfortable hugging someone and who do you feel comfortable hugging? Is such a greeting or good-bye appropriate for business associates? How does the amount of space between interactants impact a conversation? How much space do you like to have? What does standing closer to someone during a conversation indicate to you? How much of our nonverbal or affectionate behavior is culturally determined and how much is individually determined? How do you feel when you see two men and/or two women hugging? What happens when someone we are interacting with is on a different time orientation than our own? How do we respond? Why? What do these feelings tell us about the attitudes and behavior rules of our respective cultures? -About our individual attitudes?

Exercise 5.2: Seeing and Perceiving. This activity can be used in conjunction with Anderson's article on the cues of culture. It illustrates one cue of culture -- gaze -- and its impact on interaction and the meaning we ascribe to direct or indirect eye contact. Students will understand how they have come to interpret eye contact in culturally specific ways and how misunderstandings can arise when we misinterpret a person's intentions or level of interest based on the amount of eye contact they use. Divide students into groups of four. The groups are to engage in a directed discussion that will hopefully lead to a decision being made. Each group will receive four slips of paper with each slip having one of the following messages:

1. You are an African-American and one of several managers in a large, multinational firm. You have asked a group of other managers to come together to generate ideas for the company's upcoming Employee Appreciation Day. You would like the group to come to a decision as to where the festivities will take place and what types of food and entertainment will be provided. Your job is to engage all group members in a discussion of the available alternatives. You and the other three managers all hold the same level of position. You engage in a lot of direct eye contact while talking, but much less eye contact when listening to a person. (*Do not attempt to use accented speech or reveal the country or culture that you are from.)

2. You are from Japan and one of several managers in a large, multinational firm. You have been asked to join a group of managers to discuss plans for the upcoming Employee Appreciation Day. You hold the same level of position as the other three group members. You engage in a lot of indirect eye contact when speaking and listening to people. (*Do not attempt to use accented speech or reveal the country or culture that you are from.)

3. You are a Caucasian from the United States and one of several managers in a large, multinational firm. You have been asked to join a group of managers to discuss plans for the upcoming Employee Appreciation Day. You engage in a lot of direct eye contact when listening to people but a moderate amount when speaking to people. (*Do not attempt to use accented speech or reveal the country or culture that you are from.)

4. You are from Saudi Arabia and one of several managers in a large, multinational firm. You have been asked to join a group of managers to discuss plans for the upcoming Employee Appreciation Day. You hold the same level of position as the other three group members. You engage in a lot of direct eye contact while speaking and your gaze is long, intense, and unbroken. (*Do not attempt to use accented speech or reveal the country or culture that you are from.)

Each group member receives one of the above four roles. Give the students time to read their roles and understand what their instructions are. The member who has called the meeting should begin the discussion and give the group a short synopsis of why they have been called together. Allow the role play to continue for approximately fifteen to twenty minutes.

Engage the class in a discussion of what happened during the exercise. Questions for discussion: Was it difficult to role play the nonverbal behavior of a culture other than your own? What nonverbal behavioral differences did you notice among the group members? With whose nonverbal behavior did you feel comfortable? Why? With whose did you not? Why? Could you guess the culture of each individual? Did your perceptions of their nonverbal behavior match their intentions while behaving? What discrepancies were there between the sender's nonverbal behavior and the receiver's perception of the behavior? What communication problems occurred as a result of the different types of eye contact used? Can you think of times when you have felt uncomfortable with another person's nonverbal behavior (eye contact, touch, proximity, etc.)? What meanings did you ascribe to their behavior and did this meaning match their intentions? How can we become more comfortable with the nonverbal behavior of other cultures and co-cultures?

Exercise 5.3: When Another Is Silent. This activity deals with silence as a nonverbal behavior and is designed to be used with McDaniel's article on Japanese nonverbal communication as a reflection of Japanese culture. Most people have experienced a conversation where one person did most of the talking while the other took the "patient listener" role. Such experiences can lead to feelings of frustration and, sadly, sometimes to the end of developing relationships. On the other hand, it is also common to feel responsible for carrying the conversation with little assistance from a more silent friend or acquaintance. While both people in a conversation may have the responsibility of "monitoring" the extent to which they are sharing information and listening to the other share, striking a comfortable balance between the two is not always implicitly agreed upon by all individuals. The extent to which we speak and use silence in a conversation is often culturally determined.

What counts as a balance between listening and talking may be culturally determined. As has been mentioned in several articles in the *Reader*, we learn as we grow up the cultural norms of interaction. Conversational competence in one culture may include asking many questions while in another, such communicative behavior would be deemed intrusive. This case study focuses on how different cultures perceive conversation competence during the first stages of a potential romantic relationship. Read the case and answer the questions that follow. As you read, consider your own experiences on first dates: What happened? How did you interpret the other person's communication?

Jonathan and Noriko were out on their first date together. They had met in one of their classes and talked with each other several times at school. On the way over to the movie theater Jonathan noticed that Noriko was rather quiet, more quiet than when he had talked with her at school. After the movie, Jonathan suggested that they have coffee at a local cafe. Noriko still did not say very much as they sipped their coffee and Jonathan found himself filling in the silences with comments about school and questions about her family and growing up in Japan. He also talked a lot about his family since he was very close with them. Even though she answered his questions with short responses and didn't seem very willing to say much about her family, Noriko appeared to be in good spirits and when asked, said she was having a good time.

Jonathan dropped Noriko off at her apartment at about 11:00. They said goodnight at her door and as Jonathan got in his car, he was convinced Noriko had had a terrible time. He was worried that she hadn't said very much throughout the evening and wondered if he had offended her in some way. He talked with Noriko just before their class a few times the following week but they didn't make any plans to go out again. About a month later, after the school year had ended, Jonathan found out from a mutual friend that Noriko was disappointed that they never went out again. She said that she had really enjoyed his company and was hoping they could see each other again.

Questions for discussion: From the information above, describe the communication styles of Noriko and Jonathan. Why had Jonathan and Noriko perceived the success of their first date so differently? How might their relationship have developed differently? What could each have done to continue its development? What does quiet or silence communicate to you on a first date? Where did you get this interpretation(s)? Consider some alternative interpretations of silence. How does context and familiarity influence how we interpret their quietness or silence? Describe a time when a person you had just begun dating or had just met wasn't saying very much. How did you interpret this person's silence? Did you find out what this silence meant to this person?

Exercise 5.4: Culture and Conversation. To some people, conversation can be understood as an art form. Others may see it as purely functional, merely words that accomplish a set goal. How we approach conversation with other people can depend a great deal on how we have been acculturated to use and orient ourselves toward social discourse. Conversation and interpersonal relations are synonymous: when we converse we are relating interpersonally-*person to person*. And as we know, conversation includes more than spoken words. The use of silence and space, and the conceptualization of time, also make up the "stuff" of conversation.

This activity may be used with both Dolphin and Hall's articles and illustrates how the use of space, silence, and time during conversation can greatly affect intercultural relations and perceptions of other cultures. Ask students to read each of the conversational descriptions given below and envision a scenario where members from both cultures are engaging in conversation. This exercise can also be done by using the descriptions below in a dialogue and having two or more students role play an interaction in front of the class.

Culture A

Talking is synonymous with productivity in this culture. When one talks with another, something useful and functional is taking place. If there is talk, then something is being accomplished. Periods of silence are not looked upon favorably, are perceived as awkward moments, and generally a waste of time because silence makes use of time in an unproductive way.

If people are not talking, questions are asked or the subject is changed in an attempt to continue the flow of words. Curt, hurried language is the norm. Conversation in this culture is also marked by considerable distance (approximately three feet) between two individuals. It is considered extremely rude to "get in people's faces."

Culture B

This culture views talk as something quite special, not to be overused for fear it may be tread upon or misused. Talk is not how a person displays wisdom or shows the "true" self. "The one who talks knows little and reveals only falsehoods" is a common saying. Silence is what wise people engage in because knowledge lies within the individual, not on the outside. People respect intuition and introspection.

When members of this culture do talk, they are brief but clear, simple but eloquent. Words are unique objects that must be used carefully and after much consideration. The more interpersonal distance between two people talking, the less likely the conversation will end in agreement or satisfaction for both parties. People in this culture stand and sit very closely as they converse in order to better understand each others' "true" self.

After students have read or heard the conversation, ask them to consider some of the following questions in small groups or as a large class: How did you perceive each culture? Which cultural way of engaging in conversation do you most identify with and why? Which characteristics of each culture comprise your own conversational style? What difficulties might arise when people from these two cultures attempt to engage in conversation? What can people do to prevent these difficulties? Think of an intercultural conversation that you engaged in that included some of the nonverbal differences between Culture A and B. How did you deal with the differences then and would you deal differently with them now?

Exercise 5.5: Time and Culture. The following case study is designed to be used with Hall's article on time and demonstrates the difficulties people can encounter when learning and adapting to how individuals from other cultures perceive and orient to time. How time is viewed in some cultures is not a **fixed** orientation but can fluctuate depending on the context and the individual.

When people conceptualize time differently, their relationships may be affected. Ask students to read the story below and answer the questions that follow. The narrator is a teacher from the United States teaching in the African country of Malawi.

I had arranged to meet Paul at 2:00 on Saturday in front of the post office. I had been invited by his mother for tea and he was meeting me to take me to their home in the hills surrounding the small town I called home for two years. Paul was an older student who started Form One (freshman) when he was 26. Being the oldest in the family, he had been needed at home and could not attend school until he was a young man. I was looking forward to meeting his family.

I arrived at the post office at 1:00. Because it was Saturday, there were not many people in town. The busiest days were Mondays and Thursdays--market days--and the weekends tended to bring fewer people into town during the day. As I waited for Paul, I watched the people come and go as they checked their mailboxes. 2:15 came and still no Paul. I was beginning to wonder whether I had heard 2:00 or 3:00 when Paul and I spoke the day before. I was sure it was 2:00. 2:30 came and I was beginning to get frustrated. 2:45 came and now I was angry. Why did he say 2:00 and then not show up?

As my watch clicked to exactly 2:56, 1 saw Paul turn the comer of one of the several butchers in town. He approached the post office, smiled, and greeted me.

"It's a long walk to my home. I hope you're ready for a journey."

I said yes, half-waiting for an apology from him for being late. It never came.

"Paul, did you say you would meet me at 2:00 or 3:00?"

"I said 2:00. 1 hope you were not waiting long. Are you ready to go?"
Still no apology or explanation. After a very long walk we reached his home. The afternoon was wonderful and I thoroughly enjoyed meeting Paul's family. When I returned to school the following Monday, I asked one of the Malawi teachers what she would have thought about Paul arriving almost an hour late.

"Oh, but he was not late. You said he came at 2:56. That's still 2:00."

"It's a lot closer to 3:00 than 2:00," I responded.

"Ah, perhaps in 'American time' but remember here we are on 'African time.'"

Some questions for discussion in either small groups or as a class: How had the U.S. teacher understood "African time"? How would you describe African time? American time? Do you think the U.S. teacher should have been upset with Paul? Would you have left town? Would you have said something to Paul about arriving at 2:56? What might you have said? Can you identify and describe an event during a relationship that you have had, intercultural or

94

intracultural, that was affected by differing conceptualizations of time? How did you respond to this difference and why did you respond this way? How might you respond now under similar circumstances? Any changes?

Test Items for Chapter 5

Multiple Choice

1. Nonverbal behaviors that consist of body movements, gestures, and facial expressions are categorized as
    a. chronemics.
    b. proxemics.
    c. kinesics.
    d. paralanguage.

2. Differences between Arab cultures in which people tend to stand closely together when speaking and North American cultures in which people carry on conversation at a distance of eighteen to thirty-six inches are differences in
    a. olfactics.
    b. vocalics.
    c. haptics.
    d. proxemics.

3. Nonverbal behaviors that communicate warmth and closeness are referred to as _____ behaviors.
    a. contact
    b. immediacy
    c. collective
    d. internal

4. Cultures that display a high degree of "expressive" behaviors have been labeled as
    a. high-contact cultures.
    b. masculine.
    c. interdependent.
    d. individualistic cultures.

5. In a low-context culture, most of the information is contained within
    a. the physical context of the message.
    b. the person sending a message.
    c. the person receiving a message.
    d. the explicit message itself.

6. According to McDaniel, which cultural trait lessens Japanese reliance on verbal exchange?
   a. vague statements
   b. empathy *
   c. ambiguity in conversations
   d. None of the above

7. Hand gestures are never used in Japan in reference to a person who is present at the time because:
   a. It is against Confucian ethics.
   b. The Japanese do not use any nonverbal gestures.
   c. This reduces the opportunity for offending anyone present and sustains harmony. *
   d. None of the above.

8. By avoiding eye contact, Japanese participants:
   a. evince an air of humility and sustain *wa*. *
   b. exercise power.
   c. indicate disagreement.
   d. None of the above.

9. The Japanese attitude toward personal space is contradictory because
   a. they are passive about personal space but active about office space.
   b. in uncrowded situations they maintain their personal space, but in crowded situations they do not resist contact with strangers. *
   c. they strive to maintain greater personal space with Americans but less personal space with Hispanics.
   d. None of the above.

10. The Japanese proclivity for conservative dress styles and colors emphasizes
    a. the nations value of lapel pins and uniforms.
    b. the nations value of status.
    c. the nations value of collectivism. *
    d. All of the above.

11. In Hall's discussion of proxemics, the distance associated with business transactions and professional exchanges is called the _____ zone.
    a. intimate
    b. personal
    c. social
    d. public

12. Which of the following is NOT a predictor of social distance according the Schmitt's 1972 study?
    a. cultural distance
    b. status
    c. social identity
    d. power

13. Dolphin argues that several variables other than culture may predict interpersonal distance. Which of the following is NOT one of the variables she describes?
    a. ethnicity
    b. gender
    c. the environment
    d. language

14. Territory differs from personal space in that
    a. personal space is bigger than territory.
    b. territory has stable, definable boundaries and personal space is transient.
    c. animals other than humans inhabit territory.
    d. personal space encompasses the concept of territory.

15. Monochronic time is characterized by
    a. doing several tasks at once.
    b. the need for a strong leader.
    c. doing one thing at a time.
    d. the lack of a large bureaucracy.

16. Hall concludes about P-time and M-time that
    a. P-time is superior to M-time.
    b. M-time has more advantages than P-time.
    c. P-time users cannot learn to understand M-time.
    d. P-time and M-time do not

True/False

    T 1. Nonverbal messages tell us how to interpret verbal messages.
    F 2. People typically make conscious choices about their nonverbal behavior.
    T 3. Nonverbal communication is subject to cultural variation.
    T 4. Contact cultures are generally located in warm countries and low-contact cultures in cool climates.
    F 5. People in individualistic cultures are less nonverbally affiliative than people in collectivist cultures.
    F 6. We can learn to read people's nonverbal behaviors like a book given an understanding of where they fall along the dimensions of masculinity, collectivism, and context.

F   7.   When confronted with out-group members, Japanese can be quite expressive and display considerable nonverbal affiliativeness.

T   8.   Self-restraint of body movement in out-group environments by the Japanese is designed to avoid attention and maintain situational harmony or balance.

F   9.   Japanese children experience little touch from their mothers and this non-touch standard continues into adulthood.

T   10.   For the Japanese, laughter can signal joy, disguise embarrassment, sadness, and anger.

F   11.   P-time and M-time are the same across cultures.

T   12.   Members of typically polychronic time cultures can adapt to monochromic time.

Essay Questions

1. Anderson claims that "culture is primarily a nonverbal phenomenon." How does he support his argument?
2. Differentiate between individualism and collectivism as they refer to dimensions of nonverbal communication and culture.
3. What does Anderson mean when he indicates that some cultures are masculine while others are feminine?
4. What accounts for the finding that in individualistic countries like the United States, small talk, flirting, and dating are more important than in more collectivistic cultures?
5. Briefly define and give an example of the intercultural dimension of "power distance."
6. Referring to at least two different articles, differentiate between high- and low-context cultures.
7. Explain how social balance affects nearly all Japanese nonverbal behavior.
8. What does McDaniel mean by the "thematic consistency concept" in regard to culture?
9. Differentiate between personal space and territory and provide an example of each.
10. Personal space has been described in terms of a "bubble" and an "electrical field." Which do you think is the most descriptive and why?
11. What relationship, if any, exists between age and personal space?
12. What impact does the physical environment have on norms of personal space across cultures?
13. Differentiate between Hall's conceptions of monochromic and polychronic time. In your discussion, provide specific examples of each.
14. Identify two advantages and two disadvantages of monochromic time.
15. Identify two advantages and two disadvantages of polychronic time.
16. What is the relationship between gender and perception of time?
17. What is the relationship between high- and low-context cultures and M-time and P-time?
18. When communicating interculturally, why would it be important to take into consideration both intentional and unintentional forms of nonverbal communication?

Chapter 6
Cultural Context: The Influence of the Setting

Chapter Synopsis

After reading this chapter, students will be more aware of the influence of culture on contexts such as small group communication in the workplace, discussion and negotiation strategies, counseling situations, health care, and the classroom. Students should be able to make connections between their own experiences of communicating within each of the contexts discussed in the readings and compare their own cultural expectations with those articulated by the authors. This chapter offers students some practical application of the concepts presented in the previous two chapters.

In McDaniel and Samovar's article, which examines the cultural convergence of Japanese, American, and Mexican employees in Maquiladora plants, students will be introduced to some of the "real life" consequences of cultural differences in the realm of intercultural business. Friday continues this theme by examining German and American managers' discussion behaviors. Stefani, Samovar, and Hellweg provide an overview of cultural variations in negotiation styles also relevant to international business and politics. This article offers students a collection of perspectives and is not limited to a comparison of two cultures. Chen and Chung examine the role of Confucianism on organizational communication in Hong Kong, Japan, Singapore, South Korea, and Taiwan.

Cathcart and Cathcart provide an historical description of the Japanese conception of the group and describe the relationships between tradition and current business and family practices. This article in particular offers students insight into the ways in which historical and geographical developments in a particular culture can shape people's day-to-day interactions. Geist offers a particularly insightful discussion of the role of intercultural issues in the health care setting. Students may be encouraged to explore the ongoing health care debates in this country within an intercultural framework. Finally, Stefani explores cultural diversity in the learning environment. Students will come to understand the necessity of acculturation assessment instruments in todays diverse classrooms. Additionally they will become familiarized with numerous cultural variations in learning styles, problems with language diversity, and the impact of culture on gender and the classroom.

Discussion Ideas

1. McDaniel and Samovar indicate that the most important aspect in international business and transnational corporations is to have managers possess an awareness of and appreciation for cultural variation within their labor force. Using the article, identify some of the ways owners and managers of the maquiladoras tried to accommodate diversity within the organization. Were their efforts successful? Where did they fall short? What recommendations would you make for improvement?

2.   What is the influence of the American sense of "fair play" on decision making between German and American managers? If you were asked to help design a training program for a U.S. company that consistently engaged in business with Germany, what recommendations would you make after reading Friday's article?

3.   What are the five positive behaviors identified by Stefani, Samovar, and Hellweg that can contribute to a successful business negotiation? Do you agree? What other contributory behaviors can you think of?

4.   Chen and Chung indicate that Asian nations, Japan included, have been experiencing what is called an "economic miracle." However, Japan has experienced a "no-growth economy for the last four years." Despite this being the longest slump in Japan's postwar history, "the unemployment rate among Japanese men between the ages of 30 and 55 is all but 2.1 percent" (Powell, 1995, p. 98). Explain the no-growth economy and the low unemployment percentage considering the impact of Confucianism on organizations. How does this impact communication?

5.   According to Cathcart and Cathcart's article, the Japanese believe that "the gulf that separates one people from the next is always, at base, unbridgeable." That is to say, "no foreigner in Japan can ever be completely accepted no matter how well the language is spoken to cultural nuances understood." What are the ramifications for intercultural communication?

6.   Identify two cultural differences with regard to health care that may impede proper diagnosis and treatment. Then make recommendations about how to alleviate the problems that may occur. Why is it important that health care workers in the United States learn about a variety of folk medicine practices?

7.   Why should we adapt classroom communication, structure, and learning styles to accommodate culturally diverse students? Or should we insist on conformity? What are the benefits of both? Drawbacks? How will this adaptation or conformity affect students as they graduate and move into the workforce?

Exercises

Exercise 6.1: Classroom Visitors. This activity is designed to give students a much more in-depth understanding of the role that culture plays in the business, health care, and classroom contexts and applies to all the articles in this chapter. It allows students to listen to and ask questions of business professionals, health care providers, and teachers. Students will acquire some "real life" understanding of the consequences of culture in the realm of business. Further, students will gain insight into how interaction between patients and health care workers can be affected by different perceptions of how illness should be prevented and treated. Students will also be able to talk with teachers about how culture impacts the school classroom in the United States.

This activity can be accomplished in two ways. First, students can interview someone in the business, healthcare, or educational context, ask the questions below, and then report their findings to the class. A second option is for you to invite members from all three contexts to visit your classroom. Invite two or three business professionals to your class. These visitors can be contacted via personal affiliations, local business communities, or through businesses that have a partnership with your college or university. As your visitors to address changes in the business environment due to culture. How have the personal cultural demographics of the organization changed over the last five/ten years? What cultural sensitivity training is being done? What adaptations/accommodations have been made due to increased cultural diversity in the workplace? Have office arrangements, space, time usage, uniforms, etc. been altered? Negotiations? Group dynamics? What difficulties arise in the multicultural organization?

Next, invite two or three health care workers (nurses, doctors, public health workers, counselors, etc.) to your class. These visitors can be contacted on your college or university campus or from the surrounding community. Such health care facilities as Planned Parenthood, womencare and community clinics, hospices, local hospitals, and the health department in your city are excellent possible resources. Ask your visitors to address the role that culture and cultural sensitivity have in their jobs and share some of their experiences with their clients and patients who come from different cultures. What are some of the difficulties that they had to face? How are their intercultural interactions enjoyable and stimulating? What strategies do they use to help their clients? How successful are they? What suggestions do they have for improving relations between culturally different patients and health care workers?

Finally, invite two or three K-12 teachers to your class. These visitors can be contacted at local schools throughout your community. Invite teachers who teach in a multicultural school and who are culturally diverse among themselves. Other resources are the local school districts in your community. They may be able to direct you to individuals in charge of multicultural programs and multicultural specialists at certain schools. Ask your visitors to address the influence that culture has in the classroom and share some of the experiences they have had with their students. Ask them to describe the cultural backgrounds of their students and the different learning styles to which their students are accustomed. What are the specific needs of students who come from different cultures? What difficulties arise in a multicultural classroom? What aspects do they particularly enjoy and find rewarding? What strategies do they use to teach children from different cultures? How are non-English speaking students assisted in their school and classroom?

Invite students to ask the speakers questions. This activity can also be done with visitors from the business, health care, and education professions sharing the same class period. A debriefing session during the class session after the visits would be helpful to allow students to discuss some of their own thoughts about the visitors and the impact of culture on context. Possible questions for discussion: What are your own cross-cultural experiences in the business, health care or educational environment? Do you think our society addresses the issue of cultural differences in the business, healthcare, or classroom environment(s) enough? Give examples of how U.S. society has conceptualized and administered business, healthcare, and education from a mono-cultural perspective. Give examples of how U.S. society has attempted to adapt to cultural diversity in the business, healthcare, and educational settings. What type of training could you suggest for business professionals, health care providers, and educators to make them more aware of cultural differences and the need to be sensitive to these differences?

Exercise 6.2: Differences in the Workplace. This activity is designed to accent the articles by McDaniel and Samovar, Friday, and Stefani, Samovar, and Hellweg. The workplace can be an environment where cultural differences are made distinct and obvious. We do not shed our cultural make-up and don an impartial, neutral "company culture" when we walk through the doors of a new work environment. People bring their communication styles and other cultural *modus operandi* with them when they begin a job. Respecting these ways of being and communicating, and learning how to adapt to differences in the workplace, is often a challenge. Being "equal" does not mean communicating with everyone in exactly the same way. One might say that equal respect. opportunity, and consideration are all part of what "equality" truly means.

This exercise asks students to consider situations in the workplace that might challenge their traditional way of communicating. Two hypothetical scenarios are given below. Ask students to read each scenario and answer the questions that follow. Encourage them to consider as many issues and variables that might arise in both scenarios. The last question for each scenario asks students to share their responses with another classmate. Engage students in a class discussion by asking them to share some of their responses.

Scenario #1
A Cultural Meeting

You are a female and have been requested by your supervisor to conduct an important meeting for your company. This meeting will include members of a company with whom you wish to do business. It is very important that you present your own company in a favorable light and obtain the trust of the other company's negotiation team. Ten days before the meeting you are told that the members of the visiting negotiation team consists of Germans, Japanese, and Mexicans.

1. What considerations and alterations, if any, must you make in your negotiation approach to ensure a successful meeting?
2. Why did you choose to make the changes that you did?
3. Share and compare your responses with those of a classmate. If possible, share and compare your response with a classmate who is from one of the other three cultures. What does he/she think of your responses? What did he/she consider that you did not?
4. How did your gender impact your considerations and alterations?
5. Did the male students proposed considerations and alterations differ from those of the female students?

Scenario #2
Challenges in the Workplace

Divide the class into six groups. Give the first three groups scenario A. Give the second three groups scenario B.

Scenario A

You are the manager of accounts payable in a medium-size corporation. You supervise ten people who have worked together for two years. You have hired a new person who will be joining your department next month. She is :

Group 1: Japanese and the only member of your staff who is from Japan.
Group 2: Mexican and the only member of your staff who is from Mexico.
Group 3: German and the only member of your staff who is from Germany.

You want to make her transition into your department smooth and you are eager to socialize her into the office culture.

1. What must you consider, if anything, as you prepare for this new employee's arrival?
2. How can you help the office staff work and interact with this new employee?
3. What resources are available to your new employee as she begins her work in your department?
4. Did the new employees gender influence your considerations?
5. Share and compare your responses with other classmates. What did they consider that you did not?

Scenario B

You are the manager of accounts payable in a medium-size corporation. You supervise ten people who have worked together for two years. You have hired a new person who will be joining your department next month. She is :

Group 4: An American and the only member of your staff who is from the U.S. The rest of your staff is Japanese.
Group 5: An American and the only member of your staff who is from the U.S. The rest of your staff is from Mexico.
Group 6: An American and the only member of your staff who is from the U.S. The rest of your staff is from Germany.

You want to make her transition into your department smooth and you are eager to socialize her into the office culture.

1. What must you consider, if anything, as you prepare for this new employee's arrival?
2. How can you help the office staff work and interact with this new employee?
3. What resources are available to your new employee as she begins her work in your department?
4. Did the new employees gender influence your consideration?
5. Share and compare your responses with other classmates. What did they consider that you did not?

Exercise 6.3: Religion and Organizational Communication This activity is designed to be used with the article by Chen and Chung and takes the students outside the classroom. Chen and Chung explain that Confucianism impacts many facets of life, including organizational communication. They argue that Confucianism is the major cultural factor that explains the economic success of the Asian Five Dragons. This activity examines the effects various religions might have on organizational communication and economic success.

Divide the students into groups and assign each group a specific religion - Judaism, Buddhism, Christianity, Catholicism, Taoism, Islam, Hinduism, etc. Each group will examine their specified religion using the information in the reader as well as other sources. Their objective is to determine how the religion has or might impact organizational communication and how religion might determine the economic success of its members and the culture as a whole. Have the groups report their findings to the class.

Exercise 6.4: The story of Judy Evans and Mrs. Mamoud. This case study can be used with the article on healthcare by Geist. It asks the students to imagine themselves as Judy Evans, a recently graduated physiotherapist who has traveled to Singapore to take her first appointment in a general hospital. She has read books on Singapore history and culture as well as current health problems and health care services in Singapore in order to prepare for the job. Judy is committed to gaining more knowledge and understanding of the people and intends to learn the language. Have the students read the following case study and answer the questions that follow using the information gained from Geist's article.

The Story of Judy Evans and Mrs. Mamoud (Mullavey-O'Byrne, 1994, 175).

It was my first day at the hospital. The morning had gone well and I had been involved in all the things I had anticipated that I would do on my first day: meeting the staff, going on a tour of the outpatient clinic, seeing some of the treatments used frequiely in the clinic, and getting a general idea of the organization of the physiotherapy part of the service. I was very impressed with what I saw. The staff were using up-to-date techniques and state-of-the-art technology. I had not expected to find quite the level of sophisticated technology I was seeing. The clinic appeared very much like the large outpatient clinics where I had done some of my clinical placements back home.

The staff came from a variety of countries and cultural groups, which included Hong Kong, China, Malaysia, and India as well as Singapore, Australia, Canada, and England. The senior physiotherapists, S Singaporean Chinese who had completed her physiotherapy course in England, referred to her staff as "her international family of physiotherapists." Everyone was very eager to find out about me, my interests, my family, and why I had come to Singapore.

After lunch I was feeling reasonably comfortable in my new environment and eager to start treating my patients. I was very aware of the numbers of people who were arriving to have treatments and of the large caseloads carried by individual staff. I was determined not to increase their workload by asking for assistance. I had listened attentively to the senior physiotherapist when she had been orienting me to the clinic. As well as taking note of the routines in the clinic, I had also formed a good idea about the location of equipment and supplies.

When the senior physiotherapists informed me that another staff member would be assisting me with my afternoon caseload, I was quick to reply that this would not be necessary. I was sure I could manage. She did not respond directly to me, but smiled and wished me a successful afternoon. She added that she would be in a clinical meeting for 1 hour and would speak to me again after she returned to her office.

I was full of confidence and excitement when I collected the referral card for my first patient from the reception desk. As I walked into the main treatment area I read the referral to myself: "Mamoud, Alya. Female, 32 years, married two children. Diagnosis: Painful right knee, restricted movement following car accident. Treatment: assess, mobilize."

As I called her name I tried to guess who Mrs. Mamoud might be from among the large number of people in the room. I waited a few seconds before calling her name again. This time one of the physiotherapists who was collecting her patient for treatment said, "I think Mrs. Mamoud is one of the two women in black seated on the bench behind you. I suspect that she does not understand English. You will need to go up to her and indicate that you will be treating her."

I was still feeling confident as I turned to walk over to the two women. It was then that I saw that they were totally dressed in black, with only their eyes and hands visible. An article I had read, which reported that health professionals were often culturally insensitive to the needs of Muslim women, flashed before me and I panicked. I couldn't think what to do, which is very unusual for me. I am sure that Mrs. Mamoud and her companion saw the panic written all over my face and wondered what had happened. I kept saying to myself, "How am I going to communicate to Mrs. Mamoud that I need to examine her knee, in a way that is culturally sensitive, when she and I don't even speak the same language?"

Discussion Questions

1. What are the main issues raised in Judy's story? Which appear most likely to have a cultural basis? Why?
2. Would you say that Judy's behavior indicates that she was culturally sensitive? Do you believe that the senior physiotherapist was cultural sensitive to Judy's needs? What instances from the story support your answers? Why do you see these as culturally sensitive or culturally insensitive behaviors?
3. Discuss the alternatives available to Judy when she realizes that language is a barrier

to communicating with Mrs. Mamound. Generate a list of options Judy might explore to help her carry out an initial assessment of Mrs. Mamound's knee, options that are both culturally sensitive and clinically correct.

4. What are Mrs. Mamound's possible expectations for treatment? What might be her needs, when thinking about culturally sensitive approaches to treatment? In what ways might her needs differ from those of other clients? In what ways are they similar? (Mullavey-O'Byrne, 1994, pp. 175-176)

Exercise 6.5: Education and Cultural Values This case study, Japan (Goodman, 1994, p. 132) is provided to support the education article by Stefani and Samovar and the article by Cathcart and Cathcart on Japanese groups. A discussion of the case study is presented.

Japan

Recently, a major educational joint venture was established between a prestigious U.S. business school and an equally renowned Japanese university. The purpose of the venture was to establish an American-style MBA program in Japan. Although the vast majority of students in the first year's class were Japanese, the professors and some of the students were form the U.S. school

As the first semester neared the end, the American and Japanese students had gotten over their initial shyness and were getting along very well. The examination period was approaching and one of the first exams for the year was in finance. The professor has distributed a case that would be the basis for the exam. each student was to prepare a comprehensive spreadsheet and provide exhibits to be attached to the exam. The students were free to use computers and outside reference books. All preparatory work was to be done individually, guided by the U.S. school's honor code that all students signed pledging their commitment to honesty and integrity in their work at school. While the American students were busy at the library and computer center, their Japanese counterparts were nowhere to be seen.

While grading the exams, the American professor noted the near uniformity of the answers of the Japanese students. After some further investigation, he learned that nearly every Japanese student had collaborated during their preparation for the exam in clear violation of the specific instructions of the professor and in violation of the honor code they all pledged to follow.

The American professor was dismayed by the betrayal of the students. he was even more upset by the apparent lack of concern shown by the Japanese administration The American students who quickly learned of the Japanese "conspiracy" were totally disillusioned. they realized that they could no longer trust their Japanese colleagues whom they otherwise admired for their hard work (Goodman, 1994, p. 132) .

Discussion questions
1. How do you explain the behavior of the Japanese students?
2. How do you explain the reaction of the Japanese administration?
3. How should the American professor respond to the situation?

Discussion of Japan Case Study

American society is characterized by a strong sense of individualism. . . . In societies high in individualism (the U.S.) students are expected to work on their own initiative for their personal achievement, which will be rewarded by society. . . . American children are taught that individual achievement, hard work, and fair play will lead to success.

In highly collectivist societies such as Japan, group work is idealized as the preferred method to achieve success. calling attention to oneself through individual initiative for individual rewards is not the ideal. working within the group context, whether at home, school, or work, is rewarded and leads to success.

Although teachers are honored for their knowledge, the social order of society is preserved by learning how to be an effective group member. In such societies, it is common for students to collaborate before and sometimes during tests. A student who did not cooperate by not engaging in group preparation for exams or by not letting his or her paper be seen by others would become an outcast and could not succeed within the context of the group. the future assistance of the others would be withdrawn and the stigma of not being a team player would have dramatic consequences. There have been hundreds of recorded incidents of Americans going abroad to study and being shocked by the apparent "cheating/cooperating" found in other more collectivist societies. Likewise, there have many cases in which international students coming to the United States to study found themselves quickly ostracized from their American peers because they anticipated greater sharing of information during tests and exams and were labeled as cheaters when they acted on their expectations.

In the description here, the Japanese students were acting in a perfectly appropriate manner for success in japan. likewise, the American students were acting as Americans do. The Japanese students had no way of knowing that they had created such a serious violation of trust in the eyes of Americans.

The American professor should have been prepared for this situation. granted, he is part of an American institution, but he is operating in Japan and the honor code form is not going to change a custom that the students have been socialized to perform throughout their lives (Goodman, 1994, 142-143).

Test Items for Chapter 6

<u>Multiple Choice</u>

1. In McDaniel and Samovar's article where Mexicans, Japanese, and Americans worked in the same maquiladora plant, the potential for miscommunication in the area of organizational loyalty is great because
    a. self-interest propels Mexican workers.
    b. Japanese mangers complain that both Americans and Mexicans are not loyal to the company. *
    c. Americans tend to form bonds with their managers.
    d. All of the above.

2. In regard to personal distance
    a. Mexicans interact at much greater distances than do Americans.
    b. Japanese expect greater spacial separation, but not as great as Americans.
    c. Both Mexicans and Americans interact at closer spacial distances than do the Japanese. *
    d. None of the above.

3. Tactile interaction can impact cross-cultural communication between the three cultures represented in the Maquiladora because
    a. the Japanese avoid physical expressiveness in public but Mexicans are very tactile. *
    b. the Americans are the only group that traditionally shake hands at business meetings.
    c. Mexicans engage in very little touch behavior outside the family.
    d. None of the above.

4. According to Friday, the American manager's expectation or need to be liked is in direct contrast with the German manager's need to be
    a. educated.
    b. credible. *
    c. confrontational.
    d. fair.

5. Unlike the German manager's orientation to his or her corporation, the American manager's orientation
    a. is long term.
    b. is typically formal.
    c. often consists of on-the-job training. *
    d. teaches specific rules and procedures.

6. One indication given by Friday that Germans tend to focus on the past more than their American counterparts is evidenced in the fact that
    a. German architecture is older than American architecture.
    b. Americans engaged in space exploration before the Germans.
    c. Germans tend to begin discussions with historical background information. *
    d. Americans have lower standards for higher education than their German counterparts.

7. Which is NOT a characteristic of North American negotiators?
    a. Argumentation
    b. Formality *
    c. Competition
    d. A concern for time

8. Women will find most favorable business negotiation conditions outside the U.S. in countries such as
    a. Egypt, Hong Kong, and Latin America.
    b. Germany, Israel, and Eastern Europe.
    c. Sweden, China, and Saudi Arabia.
    d. Israel, Hong Kong, and Sweden. *

9. For Latin American negotiators, a blunt "no" may
    a. destroy the established friendship. *
    b. result in immediate compliance.
    c. signify more time is needed to examine the deal.
    d. All of the above.

10. Age seniority is the single most important criterion used in the selection of team leaders in which of the following cultural groups?
    a. American
    b. Japanese *
    c. Brazilian
    d. Saudi Arabian

11. In contrast with their American counterparts, Japanese negotiators
    a. are more concerned with agreeing on principles than specific details. *
    b. would rather debate specific details first.
    c. believe that there is no relationship between principles and specifics of negotiated agreements.
    d. are likely to present their demands for agreements explicitly in the process of negotiating.

12. Which is NOT one of the principles of the teachings of Confucius?
    a. the family is the basic unit.
    b. there is an emphasis on education.
    c. self-cultivation is important. *
    d. there are heirachial relationships among people.

13. According to Chen and Chung, Confucian societies and organizations invest heavily in communication through
    a. rule learning, long-term interaction, and in-group exclusion.
    b. rule learning, personal contact, and short-term interaction.
    c. out-group exclusion, education, and innate learning.
    d. rule learning, long-term interaction, and out-group exclusion. *

14. Communication styles in Confucian based societies and organizations are often non-confrontational because
    a. intermediaries are used to initiate a relationship or resolve a conflict. *
    b. superiors do not discipline subordinates.
    c. subordinates never disagree.
    d. All of the above.

15. The first circle of the many groups that dominate Japanese life is
    a. the family. *
    b. the village.
    c. one's business.
    d. school friends.

16. The Japanese way of viewing individuals and groups is best described by which of the following statements?
    a. No individual is ever apart from a group. *
    b. Individuals make choices about the groups they join.
    c. Individual rights are highly valued in group interactions.
    d. A group is a collection of independent individuals.

17. Which of the following persons is most likely to receive a promotion in a Japanese organization?
    a. A bright young employee who was highly recruited five years ago.
    b. A woman who has been with the organization for ten years.
    c. A man who has been with the organization for seven years. *
    d. An oldest son who has been with the organization for six years.

18. In Japan, bosses are considered to be
    a. *oyabun.* *
    b. *kobun.*
    c. *ninjo.*
    d. *on.*

19. Which of the following is NOT an accurate description of the Japanese *Giri?*
    a. The concept of *giri* serves as check against factionalism.
    b. *Giri* controls the horizontal relationships in a hierarchical system.
    c. *Giri* refers to the obligation that exists between persons.
    d. *Giri* refers to the life-long relationships established in formal education. *

20. Which of the following is NOT a criticism of transcultural nursing identified by Geist?
    a. the tendency to view cultural differences as a unified whole
    b. assuming a cause-effect relationship for behaviors
    c. the perspective is too global in nature *
    d. the approach does not consider stresses of adapting to a new cultural setting

21. Negotiating cultural understanding in the health care context requires that providers and patients
    a. speak the same language.
    b. like one another.
    c. have similar approaches to treating illnesses.
    d. build a supportive and trusting relationship. *

22. Which of the following is NOT among the common beliefs regarding the cause of disease within the folk-healing belief system of *Curanderismo?*
    a. Disease is caused by natural and supernatural forces.
    b. Imbalance of hot and cold contribute to disease.
    c. Physical fatigue results in disease. *
    d. Emotions influence and may cause disease.

23. Western medical practice tends to treat patients as
    a. persons with a medical condition.
    b. people who are anxious about interacting with medical professionals.
    c. malfunctioning human machines. *
    d. individuals with imbalances of hot and cold.

111

24. According to Stefani and Samovar, educators in multicultural schools are obligated to
    a. become familiar with the educational structure of the cultural heritage of the students in the class.
    b. assess the acculturation level of each student in the class.
    c. expect less of students from other cultures.
    d. both a and b. *

25. In topic associating communication
    a. accounts focus on a single topic.
    b. communication progresses in a linear fashion.
    c. questions are not asked until the speaker is completely finished.
    d. a series of episodes are linked to some person or theme. *

26. Visual learners
    a. do not rely on word association.
    b. use mental pictures to remember.
    c. code with imagery.
    d. All of the above. *

27. According to Stefani, which is NOT a problem faced by students with limited English proficiency?
    a. They must be concerned with both linguistics and cognition.
    b. They are required to rid themselves of their native language immediately. *
    c. They often have academic delays in their native language.
    d. They enter schools in the U.S. at various grade levels.

28. Which is NOT a possible manifestation of cultural gender-roles in the classroom?
    a. gender separation
    b. academic success
    c. friendship building *
    d. risk taking

True/False

F   1.   For the Mexican worker, the base social unit includes the corporation as a part of the extended family.

T   2.   An American worker will normally express an honest, forthright opinion rather than be indirect.

F   3.   Because Americans and Mexicans are from cultures considered high-context, it is easier for them to communicate with each other rather than with the Japanese.

T   4.   According to Friday, American managers approach the business relationship more impersonally than German managers.

F	5.	German managers are more likely to be selected and promoted based on personal accomplishments than their education and credentials.
F	6.	Traditionally, German managers share the American sense of "fair play."
T	7.	American managers being trained to work with their German counterparts will best learn through interactive role plays when the focus is on debriefing the informal rules of the interaction.
T	8.	There are many countries where customs, attitudes, and religion are hostile to women in business.
F	9.	Most negotiation problems occur over specific behavioral differences rather than deep cultural misunderstandings.
F	10.	North American negotiators focus on friendships first and business second.
T	11.	American negotiators tend to be more interested in logical arguments than the people with whom they are negotiating.
F	12.	When negotiating with a person from France, it is unlikely that you will engage in debate or experience open dissent.
T	13.	American negotiators view negotiation sessions as problem-solving sessions even if no real problem exists.
T	14.	*Jen* involves benevolence, self-discipline, filial piety, brotherly love, and trust.
T	15.	In Confucian societies, many rules in interpersonal communication are transferred to the organizational setting.
F	16.	Confucian teachings specify that an effective leadership must follow the requirements of abstract role definment and sincerity.
T	17.	Japanese geography and history form a context in which to interpret Japan's concept of the group.
F	18.	Japanese women experience the group in the same way as Japanese men.
T	19.	In Japan there is no need to define groups because they are part and parcel of everyday human interaction.
T	20.	Hierarchy is the basis for all relationships in Japan.
F	21.	An ingenious young employee is likely to be promoted before a lazy employee who has been with the company five years longer.
T	22.	Cultural misunderstanding occurs when two people with different cultural orientations assume that they share the same expectations for a situation but choose different behaviors to convey their intentions.
F	23.	Western medical training programs are actively integrating intercultural communication training in their curriculum.
T	24.	The task of understanding and diagnosing medical conditions is often complicated by cultural differences.
F	25.	"Yes" always means yes across cultural boundaries.
F	26.	Social class has more influence on cognitive style than does culture.
F	27.	All cultures hold teachers in high esteem.
T	28.	Dependent learners are interested in obtaining their teachers direction and feedback.
F	29.	Field-dependent individuals are analytical and focus on abstract stimuli.

T   30.   Families that adhere to traditional religious and cultural patterns are more likely to adhere to rigid gender roles than families who have adopted bicultural patterns.

Essay Questions

1.   Identify the different authority structures and authority basis for Mexicans, Japanese, and Americans. How might these different approaches to authority impact the organization?
2.   Why were different colored smocks used in the Maquiladora plants examined by McDaniel and Samovar? What was the attitude of each cultural group toward these different colored smocks?
3.   How is formality aligned with status for the Mexican and Japanese workers in the Maquiladora plants described by McDaniel and Samovar?
4.   Compare and contrast the German and American manager's focus with regard to their orientation to cooperation and relationship to business.
5.   Indicate how differences in education, learning styles, and problem solving between German and American managers may influence their managerial styles.
6.   What does Friday mean by the term "guidance system" and of what importance is it to his discussion of German and American managers?
7.   Define the German term *Besprechung*.
8.   What difference might it make that American managers are more oriented toward the future than German managers who are grounded in their past tradition?
9.   If you were asked to help design a training program for a U.S. company that consistently engaged in business with Germany, what recommendations would you make after reading Friday's article?
10.   List some of the cultural variations in the selection of negotiators identified by Stefani, Samovar, and Hellweg, and explain why these criteria might be used.
12.   Identify and explain the four cultural values that are often the root of cross-cultural problems at the negotiation table as identified by Stefani, Samovar, and Hellweg.
13.   Explain how the pace at which negotiations move is directly related to the decision-making process.
14.   What are the five positive behaviors identified by Stefani, Samovar, and Hellweg that can contribute to a successful business negotiation?
15.   How do the four key principles of the teachings of Confucius impact organizational communication according to Chen and Chung?
16.   What is M theory and how does it affect management?
17.   In what way did the *Shogunates* or ruling families contribute to the current Japanese conception of group?
18.   Compare and contrast the American concept of group with that of the Japanese conception of group as articulated by Cathcart and Cathcart.
19.   What is the impact of geography on the development of the Japanese conception of group?
20.   Compare and contrast the Japanese conception of group before and after the American occupation and establishment of a constitution guaranteeing individual rights. Include a discussion of *Nihinjin-ron* in your response.
21.   Differentiate between the role of Japanese men and women in groups.

22. What is the relationship between formal education and business in the Japanese culture? How is this similar or different from American culture?
23. Define the system known as the *oyaban-kobun* relationship and describe its relevance to the employer-employee relationship.
24. Compare and contrast the *yakuzi* with traditional, main-line Japanese groups.
25. Define and provide an example of "transcultural nursing."
26. Identify two cultural differences with regard to health care that may impede proper diagnosis and treatment. Then make recommendations about how to alleviate the problems that may occur.
27. Why is it important that health care workers in the United States learn about a variety of folk medicine practices?
28. Describe the Hispanic folk-healing beliefs referred to as *Curanderismo and* the practices that are central to this belief system.
29. Discuss the problems of translation that may occur in a health care setting. Include a discussion of the choice of translator.
30. What are the three categories of learning styles articulated by Stefani? Pick one category and describe two orientations within the category.
31. Distinguish between students intrinsic and extrinsic motivation to learn.
32. In what ways might teachers improve interaction and promote learning in a classroom of linguistically diverse students?
33. How does culture establish gender role norms in the classroom?

Chapter 7
Communicating Interculturally: Becoming Competent

Chapter Synopsis

Chapter 7 represents a shift in the orientation of the *Reader* from raising awareness of similarities and differences between and across cultures toward practical advice for communicating interculturally. Articles in this chapter address both problems and solutions in a variety of intercultural contexts. Descriptions of and suggestions for competent communication interculturally are offered. After reading this chapter, students should be more prepared to actually engage in intercultural communication rather than simply talk about it.

In the first essay, Barna describes six factors that often result in communication breakdowns across cultural boundaries. In addition, she offers suggestions on ways students might turn stumbling blocks into building blocks for more effective communication with members of other cultures. Spitzberg provides students with a complex model of the interculturally competent communicator. Students will be able to identify ways they can increase their own communicative competence. Ting-Toomey focuses on the specific context of intercultural conflict. Her essay offers students a framework within which to understand cultural differences in the event of interpersonal conflict, but also suggests a series of skills that can be helpful in managing conflict when it occurs in the intercultural encounter.

Young Yun Kim addresses the challenges of adapting to a new culture. This article may be particularly insightful to students in your class who are currently in the process of acculturation. Finally, Sauceda introduces students to the concept of multicultural understanding through aesthetic communication. An examination of aesthetic approaches such as performance study, rainbow voices, theatre, dance, painting, film, and music reveal the intercultural benefits of pursuing aesthetic communication.

Discussion Ideas

1. What does Barna mean when she talks about an "assumption of similarity"? What are some of the implications of upholding such an assumption? Do you agree that assumptions of similarity are problematic to intercultural interactions? Are they ever useful?

2. List and describe the three major features of a competent communicator according to Spitzberg's model. Differentiate between the evaluation criteria of appropriateness and effectiveness. What happens when a person is appropriate, but not effective? Effective but not appropriate? Neither appropriate nor effective?

3. What is the relationship between low- and high-context cultures and cultures that are primarily individualistic or collectivistic with regard to approaches to conflict?

Differentiate between the role of third-party intervention in individualistic, low-context cultures and collectivistic high-context cultures. Why would it be important in a high-context culture to have an impartial mediator?

4. Young Yun Kim asserts that "no stranger's adaptation to a new culture can ever be complete no matter how long he or she interacts with the host environment." To what extent do you agree or disagree with her conclusion?

5. The underlying message of Sauceda's article is "personal action" and turning aesthetic communication into empowering strategies that create community. Why has this been so difficult to achieve? What progress is being made? Do you agree with his notion of aesthetic communication bridging cultural communities? Why or why not? What other examples of aesthetic communication in art forms are you aware of that Sauceda does not include (movies, plays, art, etc.)?

Exercises

Exercise 7.1: Improving Ourselves. This activity incorporates all of the articles in chapter 7 and focuses on the communicative behavior of students and, specifically, those aspects of their behavior that they would like to change. This activity uses the concepts in the articles in chapter 7 as a backdrop (stumbling blocks, competence, conflict, work force diversity, acculturation, and aesthetic communication) for improving intercultural communication. Using the articles in chapter 7 as a starting point, students will be given an opportunity to verbalize and develop strategies for a particular characteristic of their communicative behavior that they view as a weakness or "problem area." Begin by asking students to come prepared for the next class period with one aspect of their communicative behavior that they see as problematic or that needs "fixing." Encourage them to talk to their friends or family and solicit their opinions. But the students must agree with their opinions since there is a tendency for people not to make an effort to change if they don't see a problem. Have students answer the following questions:

a. Describe this communicative behavior that you would like to change.
b. Give one example when you communicated in this way. Include the other interactant's response to your behavior.
c. What strategy can you think of that will remedy this behavior?

When students come to the following class period, ask them to break into small groups. Each group member should share what they have written, ask the group for feedback about the strategy developed, and solicit other possible strategies. Each student should walk away from his or her group with a list of strategies. Regroup as a class and have students share some of their areas for change. The instructor should act as a probing questioner: What can you do to improve your communication with others? What will you do? How will you know if you have been successful? What affect will this improvement have on your relationships with other people?

Engage the class in a discussion on how their specific communication problems might affect their ability to be competent intercultural communicators. How might their behavior be perceived by individuals from other cultures? How would working on this one communicative behavior enhance their effectiveness as intercultural communicators? Hopefully the discussion will begin to address the issue of becoming interculturally competent through improving one's own communication with others. Encourage students to use some of the strategies offered. An assignment could even be given that asks them to document their attempts at actively applying one or more strategies.

Exercise 7.2: Stereotypes. This activity is provided as a supplement to Barna's article on stumbling blocks in intercultural communication. Stereotypes are generalizations about groups of individuals. Before even meeting someone from Africa, for example, we have "knowledge" about who that person might be because of the images that the media have shown us about Africa and its diverse people. We receive information from so many different sources it is often difficult to identify the source of our information about whole groups of people. Cultural stereotypes are not inherently negative things for they are useful for making sense of the millions of pieces of data that we collect about our world.

Stereotypes can be destructive, however, when they are based on misinformation, a lack of information, and bigotry. Using stereotypes to form intercultural relationships can be very dangerous for we do not allow individual, personal characteristics to shape our perceptions of culturally different individuals. They are especially harmful when we use them unknowingly for we can easily mistake our stereotypes for the living, breathing individual in front of us.

This exercise asks students to identify their own stereotypes about certain cultures and groups of people and consider how these stereotypes have hindered or could hinder intercultural interactions that they have had or will have. Perhaps by identifying them students will come to use them more effectively and fairly, and hopefully ignore them as they develop meaningful intercultural relationships. Students will be challenged to ask themselves difficult questions that may have surprising and possibly disturbing answers. This activity is probably most suitable for classes where a supportive, trusting environment has been maintained throughout the semester. It is also an exercise that might cause feelings of resentment and hostility from members of your class because the focus is stereotypes of cultures most likely represented by many students in your class.

For each group identified below, ask students to write down the first images that come to mind for them and the possible source of these images. Stress to students that they are compiling a list of group characteristics, not characteristics of individuals. Stereotypes are by definition composite descriptions of entire groups. Thus they should try to think "collectively" as they respond to each group. This list can be substituted for a list of your own, one that may more accurately reflect (or not reflect) the surrounding university community or your own classroom. Collect the descriptions and for the next class period, prepare a list of the students' responses. These responses can be written on the board or prepared as handouts. Use these descriptions to begin a discussion on stereotypes and their influence on intercultural interactions.

     a.   school fraternity members
     b.   blue-collar workers
     c.   women

d. Swedes
e. Muslims
f. Native-Americans
g. white males
h. gay men and women
i. African-Americans
j. Jews

Questions for discussion: Where did you get these descriptions? Media? Parents? School? Friends? Observations? Interactions? Would-you characterize these descriptions as cultural stereotypes? Why or why not? If you have had many interactions with some of these groups, are your descriptions still stereotypes? Why do we form stereotypes? When do we use them? How do we use them? Are they useful? Are they fair? When are stereotypes harmful to human interaction? When are they helpful? How could some of these stereotypes prevent positive intercultural communication with a member of one of these groups? Can you give examples when it was obvious that you were being stereotyped by another individual? Can you give examples when you were stereotyping another individual during an interaction? What was the outcome of the interaction? How did you, could you, change that outcome if you felt it necessary? What is the role of ethnocentrism in stereotyping? How do stereotypes lead to prejudice and hate? How can we prevent this from occurring?

Exercise 7.3: Intercultural Interviews. This activity takes the students out of the classroom and serves to amplify the distinction Spitzberg makes between appropriate and effective communication. Many of us may have grown up learning that you never ask a person how much salary he or she makes. Even among close friends, such a question may be considered highly inappropriate and suspicious. In cultures that believe money is sacred, a personal issue, and an indication of one's worth as an individual, such a question might be perceived as too face-threatening and private. We learn from culture what we can ask certain people and what is generally perceived as taboo topics of conversation. Such norms are very culture-specific and breaking or following them can influence the development of intercultural friendships.

This exercise will help students explore what different cultures feel is appropriate and inappropriate to discuss as well as appropriate versus effective. Ask students to interview a friend, acquaintance, or classmate who does not share their cultural background. Below is a list of suggested interview questions. Students should explain that they are interested in finding out about culturally appropriate self-disclosing behavior and that he or she may stop the interview at any time. They should let their interviewees know that it is not their intent to pry into their personal lives but rather to learn from them what they feel are appropriate topics of conversation. Their goals should be made very explicit. Afterward, students should ask this person how she or he felt during the interview. Were certain questions too personal? Is it considered appropriate in this person's culture to talk about certain topics and not others?

<u>Interview Questions</u>

1. What is your academic major?
2. In what year of school are you?
3. What kind of music do you like?
4. What is your favorite food?
5. What are some of your hobbies?
6. What is your impression of the university or college?
7. What country are you from or of which culture are you a member?
8. How would you describe your political beliefs (i.e., conservative, liberal, radical, etc.)?
9. How many family members do you have?
10. How would you describe your family?
11. Whom do you most admire?
12. What do you feel are the characteristics of a good friend?
13. What religion are you?
14. What is the most important thing in the world to you?
15. What do you think you will be doing five years from now?
16. How do you feel about your socioeconomic status?
17. When was the happiest moment in your life?
18. When was the unhappiest moment in your life?
19. What is one mistake you have made in your life?
20. What health problems do you have?

<u>Post-interview Questions</u>

Questions for the informant
1. Which questions did you not feel comfortable answering? Why?
2. Which questions would be most appropriate between people who are meeting for the first time? Between close friends? Among family members? Among romantic partners?
3. What topics do people in your culture always consider taboo in any context? What topics are considered inappropriate for discussion with certain people or in certain situations?

Questions for the students to ask themselves
1. Which questions did you feel it was inappropriate to ask this person?
2. Was there any time during the interview when you perceived the other person feeling uncomfortable? Describe what you perceived.
3. How did you respond to this person's discomfort?
4. Describe a time when you obviously broke a conversational norm unintentionally. What happened and how did culture play a role?

<u>Exercise 7.4: Individualism, Collectivism, Reward Distribution, and Conflict.</u> This activity can be used with Ting-Toomey's article on managing intercultural conflicts effectively. One area

that may result in intercultural conflict is the area of reward distribution particularly when both collectivistic and individualist cultures are involved. Ting-Toomey notes:

> In terms of the relationship between the norm of fairness and cross-cultural conflict interaction style, results from past research indicate that individualists typically prefer to use the equity norm (self-deservingness norm) in dealing with reward allocation in group conflict interaction. In comparison, collectivists oftentimes prefer to use the equality norm (the equal distribution norm) to deal with in-group members and thus avoid disharmony. (1994, p. 367)

Divide the students into two group (one group will represent collectivists and the other will represent individualists) and have the students read the case study on the next page. After reading the case study have each group draft up a distribution of money based on either their collectivist or individualists tendencies. Then have the groups role play a negotiation to resolve their distribution differences utilizing the conflict management strategies offered by Ting-Toomey.

Discussion

Individualists generally prefer an equity distribution, that is rewards based on contributions. If person A contributed 40% of the work he should receive approximately 40% of the rewards. Other people should also receive rewards based on their contributions. Person E is not likely to get much special attention from individualists in monetary terms. Instead, they might name the road after this high status person. Person F, despite his special circumstances would likely receive a share equal to his contributions. These distributions are based on the idea that it is necessary to reward individual accomplishment or the person will see little reason to work hard on the next project (Brislin, 1994). In comparison, collectivists prefer an equality distribution in which all people receive the same level of rewards. If there were five people who contributed to the project, each would receive approximately 20% of the rewards. This will keep the group functioning smoothly. The idea is that if one person gets more, it will disrupt the group. Besides the lesser contributors may contribute more on the next project. Collectivists are also more likely to give special attention to person E whose status was instrumental in acquiring the project. They are likely to vote a solid $10,000 to person E in recognition of his effort even though he does not need the money. For person F with special circumstances, they are likely to give him more than the others in the group, or to assume that person F's special needs have already been taken care of by the company separate from the distribution of the $100,000 (Brislin, 1994).

Assume that you are employed in a company (for profit) that contracts to do construction work (e.g., roads, sewage treatment facilities) in rural areas of the community where you live. The company recently received a contract for $8000,000 dollars (U.S.) to build a road. Given a number of fortunate circumstances, such as good weather, the project was completed for $7000,000. it is now the end of the fiscal year and the board of directors has decided that the extra $100,000 can be distributed the way people (who were involved in the road construction project) decide. The following people are somehow involved. All have been in the company for at least five years and get along well together.

Person A was the hardest worker and was clearly responsible for supervising a great deal of the actual day-to-day work on the project. At least 40% of the day-to-day work on the project was done by him. Persons B, C, and D were solid but not spectacular contributors. They were competent workers but not outstanding. Each contributed about 15% of the actual day-to-day work on the project. Person E is a very high status and wealthy person in the organization and in the community. Although he did not engage in any of day-to-day work on the road construction project and did not write the proposal for funding, it is known within the organization that he called upon his connections and used his influence so that the original $800,000 contract would go to the company.

Person F is a contributor much like B, C, and D. His contribution was about 15% of the work needed for the project's completion. His father died recently, however, and person F has considerable expenses associated with funeral, nursing care for his mother, and the education of his much younger brothers (his father left no estate).

Your group is unassociated with the project but has been asked to help in the decision making concerning the distribution of the $100,000. How would you distribute the money? (Brislin, 1994, pp. 80-81)

	Amount	Explanation (Why)
Person A		
Person B		
Person C		
Person D		
Person E		
Person F		
Another person		
Total = $100,000		

Exercise 7.5 Acculturation. This activity supports Kim's article on acculturation and will allow students to experience vicariously the process of acculturation. Using the information provided by Kim, students are to interview someone who has crossed cultural boundaries by entering the U.S. Depending on the diversity of the class, some students may be in the midst of the acculturation process themselves. If so, these students may share their own personal experiences or they may choose to interview someone else. The idea is to make real for the students the dramatic and all-encompassing challenges of having to construct a new life in an unfamiliar place. Some of the following questions may be helpful when conducting the interview.

1. What things have you done to help deal with the high level of uncertainty and anxiety in moving to a new culture?
2. What cross-cultural challenges have you faced since moving to the U.S.?
3. Do you feel that your adaptation has been slow?
4. What do you miss most about your original culture?
5. Do you participate in a variety of social functions in the US
6. Are you in close contact with members of your own ethnicity here in the U.S.? How large is this group?
7. Do you maintain ties with your original culture? How often?
8. Do you feel the U.S. culture has been receptive and welcoming?
9. Do you feel pressure to conform to U.S. values, attitudes and beliefs.
10. Do you speak English? Has this influenced your adaptation to the culture?
11. What changes have occurred in you as a person as a result of your moving here?
12. Do you feel these are positive changes?

Exercise 7.6 Aesthetic Communication. This activity accompanies Sauceda's article on Aesthetic communication and asks students to explore the reality of this concept. Have students individually search the media for evidence that aesthetic communication can bridge multicultural understanding. For example, students could explore book reviews, film critiques, theatre and dance companies, coverage of art exhibits, and music releases in order to find aesthetic communication forms that amplify American cultural diversity. Newspapers as well as Newsweek and Time magazines routinely carry updates on the arts, theatre, movies, etc. Have your students report their findings to the class. If time permits, the instructor may want to bring in one of the films mentioned by Sauceda for class viewing and discussion. Music samples can also be brought in, listened to, and discussed by the class. The idea is for students to gain insight into the experiences of the diverse cultures existing in America and to examine the benefits of cross-cultural collaboration in these aesthetic forms.

Test Items for Chapter 7

<u>Multiple Choice</u>

1. Suggestions for overcoming the stumbling blocks to intercultural communication include all but which of the following?
   a. learn to expect differences in nonverbal communication
   b. train ourselves to pay more attention to situational details
   c. use an investigative approach
   d. expect that there are more similarities than differences between cultures *

2. The term "cultural fatigue" is another way to talk about
   a. culture shock. *
   b. jet lag when traveling to another country.
   c. the fact that it is tiring to try to understand another culture.
   d. the stress associated with stereotypes.

3. According to Barna, cross-cultural understanding occurs when
   a. a visiting person adopts the culture of his or her present location.
   b. a third culture is created between people from different cultures. *
   c. a member of a culture adopts the cultural perspective of a visitors' native culture.
   d. two people learn to speak the same language.

4. One of the biggest stumbling blocks with respect to learning another's language according to Barna is the tendency to
   a. cling to one interpretation of a word or phrase. *
   b. be unsure of their ability to speak clearly.
   c. assume that the other is speaking too fast.
   d. forget what a word means in your native language.

5. Which of the following is NOT one of the six stumbling blocks to intercultural communication identified by Barna?
   a. misinterpreting nonverbal communication
   b. relying on stereotypical information-nation
   c. a tendency to approve or disapprove of the other
   d. assuming that their cultures are different *

6. Sets of characteristics that an individual may possess that may facilitate competent communication interaction in a normative social sense are referred to by Spitzberg as _____ systems.
   a. individual *
   b. collective
   c. episodic
   d. relational

7. Communicative competence in the intercultural setting consists of a combination of which three features?
   a. motivation, knowledge, and context
   b. skills, knowledge, and motivation *
   c. knowledge, context, and skills
   d. context, motivation, and skills

8. Which of the following statements is NOT accurate regarding a communicator's motivation?
   a. As communicator confidence decreases, motivation increases.
   b. As communicator confidence increases, motivation increases. *
   c. As communicator confidence decreases, motivation decreases.
   d. As communicator confidence increases, motivation decreases.

9. A person who is interpreted as lying, cheating, or other ethically problematic behaviors is likely to exhibit behaviors that are
   a. appropriate and effective.
   b. appropriate but not effective.
   c. effective but not appropriate. *
   d. neither appropriate nor effective.

10. Individualistic conflict negotiators are more likely to attend to which of the following issues?
    a. objective, substantive issues *
    b. relational issues
    c. socioemotional issues
    d. issues of interpretation

11. In collectivistic, high-context cultures, third party mediators are likely to be
    a. impartial parties.
    b. of lower status than the primary negotiators.
    c. a professional mediator.
    d. a person related to both parties of the dispute. *

12. Which of the following statements is most accurate?
    a. Individualistic cultures are more likely than collectivistic cultures to operate on M-time. *
    b. Individualistic cultures are less likely than collectivistic cultures to operate on M-time.
    c. Individualistic cultures are more likely than collectivistic cultures to operate on P-time.
    d. There is no relationship between individualistic and collectivistic cultures and M- or P-time.

13. Individualistic, low-context cultures are more likely to value a conflict style that
    a. is indirect.
    b. uses the equality norm.
    c. uses the equity norm. *
    d. reflects the salience of a "we" identity.

14. Which of the following is necessary to engage in a "mindfulness" state in intercultural interaction?
    a. being open to old information
    b. awareness of multiple perspectives *
    c. reinforcing existing categories
    d. thinking before speaking

15. Which of the following factors influence the rate at which newcomers adapt to a new culture?
    a. the receptivity of the host environment
    b. pressures to conform to the new environment
    c. individual predisposition to adaptation
    d. all of the above *

16. The three categories of individual conditions that may facilitate or impede acculturation include
    a. preparedness, ethnicity, and personality. *
    b. ethnicity, personality, and communication skills.
    c. mastery of the language, communication skills, and personality.
    d. preparedness, ethnicity, and mastery of the language.

17. Which of the following is NOT identified as a personality trait conducive for adaptation to a new culture?
    a. openness
    b. flexibility
    c. strength
    d. ambition *

18. According to Sauceda,
    a. 50% of America's youth describe the state of race relations in our nation as generally bad. *
    b. multicultural education should be an anti-white movement that only addresses the needs and concerns of people of color.
    c. multicultural education is about the uniqueness of distinctive groups.
    d. None of the above.

19. Which of the following is NOT an advantage of performance study?
    a. It can function as a strategy for instilling tolerance, empathy, and acceptance of culturally different groups.
    b. It can be used in so many areas.
    c. It creates linkages between art and cross-cultural understanding.
    d. It creates a singular voice within a community. *

20. Art is a form of aesthetic communication empowerment because
    a. It eliminates socially constructed oppressiveness.
    b. It allows us to discover and promote our own voices. *
    c. It allows us to focus solely on our own ethnicity.
    d. All of the above.

21. Which art form has consistently for many years confronted issues of intolerance and racial prejudice?
    a. theatre
    b. paintings
    c. dance
    d. film *

True/False

F	1.	Recognizing the fact that humans are biologically similar is of great help in learning to communicate interculturally.
T	2.	Situations that bring about emotional feeling differ from culture to culture.
T	3.	The confidence that comes with the myth of similarity is much stronger than with the assumption of differences.
T	4.	The same action can have different meanings even within a single culture.
F	5.	The effects of culture shock are universal.
T	6.	The more people believe that they are able to engage in a set of values or positive actions, the more likely they are to do so.
T	7.	As a communicator's knowledge level increases, his or her communicative competence increases.
F	8.	Continually increasing motivation will guarantee that you will be perceived as competent.
T	9.	No one culture exists exclusively at one extreme of the communication context continuum.
F	10.	M-time cultures tend to view time as more contextually based and relationally oriented.
T	11.	Every intercultural conflict consists of both substantive and relational issues.
T	12.	The higher a person is in positional power in a collectivist culture, the more likely he or she will use silence as a deliberate, cautionary conflict strategy.

F	13.	Listening is synonymous with hearing.
T	14.	Avoiding conflict does not always mean that collectivists do not care to resolve a conflict.
T	15.	Cross-cultural adaptation is achieved primarily through communication.
T	16.	Both immigrants and sojourners begin their life in a host society as strangers.
T	17.	No stranger's adaptation to a new culture can ever be complete no matter how long he or she interacts with the host environment according to Kim.
F	18.	A society marked by ethnic or cultural diversity is multicultural.
T	19.	Sauceda insists that other dimensions of our identity such as religion, age, and gender play as important a role as race.
T	20.	By learning to like the art work of various groups we may also learn to like the people they represent.
T	21.	For Cambodians, dance is the central repository for their history.

Essay Questions

1. What does Barna mean when she talks about an "assumption of similarity"? What are some of the implications of upholding such an assumption?
2. Respond to the statement that "travel, student exchange programs, joint business ventures, and so on will automatically result in better understanding and friendship."
3. Barna suggests that travelers not be provided with a list of cultural "do's" and "don'ts." What is her rationale for this suggestion and what does she suggest as an alternative?
4. One of the stumbling blocks to intercultural communication is the presence of preconceptions and stereotypes. Provide a description of each and indicate why they serve as stumbling blocks instead of building blocks.
5. What does Barna mean by the term "cultural fatigue"?
6. Differentiate between "procedural" and "substantive" knowledge, and give an example of each.
7. What does Spitzberg mean by the term "altercentrism"?
8. List and describe the three major features of a competent communicator according to Spitzberg's model.
9. Differentiate between personal, episodic, and relational systems.
10. Differentiate between the evaluation criteria of appropriateness and effectiveness.
11. How does Ting-Toomey define intercultural conflict?
12. Differentiate between "independent construal of self" and "interdependent construal of self."
13. Compare and contrast the value tendencies of individualism and collectivism.
14. What is the relationship between "in-groups" and "out-groups" and the individualism-collectivism dimension of value tendencies?
15. What is the relationship between low- and high-context cultures and cultures that are primarily individualistic or collectivistic with regard to approaches to conflict?
16. Describe the concept of "face" and its importance to understanding and engaging in intercultural conflict.
17. Identify three central issues for conflict in both individualistic, low-context cultures and

collectivistic, high-context cultures.

18. Differentiate between the role of third party intervention in individualistic, low-context cultures and collectivistic, high-context cultures.

19. Describe the concept of "mindfulness" and its relevance to managing intercultural conflicts.

20. Differentiate between the terms "acculturation" and "deculturation."

21. Provide an account for why some newcomers to a culture adapt to more quickly than others.

22. Differentiate between "personal" and "social" communication and indicate the role of each in the acculturation process.

23. What is the role of the host environment on the acculturation process?

24. To what extent are members of a host culture necessary for strangers to meet their adaptation goals?

25. Sauceda bases his article on a bicentennial "counter" celebration staged by Australian aborigines. Link this incident to his advocating aesthetic communication to enhance cultural understanding.

26. Explain Sauceda's term and metaphor "rainbow voices" as it applies to multicultural understanding.

Chapter 8
Ethical Considerations: Prospects for the Future

Chapter Synopsis

This chapter explores the issue of ethics and intercultural communication. The four articles in this chapter touch on ethical and philosophical considerations when members of diverse cultures must live together. In short, this chapter offers various perspectives on developing and improving intercultural communication so that diverse cultures can live together without destroying each other.

In the chapter's first article, Cleveland introduces students to the ethics and philosophical assumptions surrounding intercultural communication. Instead of fear and tribal loyalties, he advocates "civilization" as universal values, ideas, and practices that are accepted as useful everywhere in order to form a global civil society. Kim proposes that becoming intercultural persons with intercultural personhood is essential in order for different cultures and countries to get along. Finally, Kale's article proposes that we use the human spirit as an organizing concept for a universal value system. People of all cultures, Kale claims, have in common a human spirit that gives them the ability to make value decisions and attempt to live a fulfilling life.

Discussion Ideas

1.   Explain Cleveland's concept of civilization. Are universal laws and rules possible? Why or why not?

2.   How do we adopt Kim's notion of intercultural personhood? What characteristics do we include in this concept? Which do we exclude?

3.   What do you think of Kale's four principles that make up his universal code of ethics? Are these enough? Do you agree? What are they lacking? Principle #1 sounds like the golden rule, but how about the platinum rule? Do unto others as they would have you do unto them. Respect them the way they wish to be respected, not the way you would like to be respected. Would this be a more appropriate rule for intercultural interactions since not all cultures show respect in the same way, for the same reasons, to the same people, etc.?

Exercises

Exercise 8.1: Cultural Universals. This activity can be used with Cleveland's article on cultural diversity and asks the students to think seriously about the growing diversity in the United States as well as the idea of "wholeness incorporating diversity." Divide students into small groups and have them reread the following exert from Cleveland's article:
       . . . *civilization* is what is universal -- values, ideas, and practices that are in general
       currency everywhere, either because they are viewed as objectively "true" or because they

are accepted pragmatically as useful in the existing circumstances. These accepted "truths" offer the promise of weaving together a *civitas* of universal laws and rules, becoming the basis for a global society (1995).

After reading the exert, have students make a list of laws, rules, or practices that are generally accepted on a universal basis. (Cleveland offers, as one example, the international exchange of money). Groups must be prepared to defend the universality of these items. Additionally, have the groups create a list of laws, rules, and practices that they believe would contribute to pluralism if they were universal. Again, groups must support and defend their answers. When the groups have completed their lists, write on the board those laws, rules, and practices that were common among all groups. Have the students discuss the reality of these ideas being enacted and their effect on individual communities, the US, and the world.

Exercise 8.2: The East-West Game. This activity is an accompaniment for Kim's article on intercultural personhood or combining key attributes of the East and West. The East-West Game was originally entitled "The Emperor's Pot" and first developed by Donald Batchelder of the Experiment in International Living (Hoopes & Ventura, 1979). It simulates a negotiation session between two very different cultures. By taking part in this intercultural negotiation session, students will be able to test their ability to communicate with a culture that thinks and behaves in very different ways. The problems that often occur during intercultural communication will also be illustrated.

This activity is most useful when conducted over two or three class sessions. The exercise has been adapted to accommodate the university classroom and allow all participants to either watch or take part in the entire process. There are four phases in the activity: Phase 1--students are divided into two groups and given time to "adopt" their new culture and plan their negotiation session. Phase 11--class regroups and the negotiations begin. Phase 111--East and West meet in their own groups to discuss what happened. Phase IV--class discussion. (Phase III can be left out if there is a time constraint.)

The negotiations center on a highly coveted cultural artifact that the East has and the West wants. The West has come to the East to negotiate for the artifact. The handouts on the next two pages each team instructions for the activity.

Questions to stimulate discussion during the debriefing afterward:

1. What cultural traits characterized your culture?
2. What traits did you notice in the other culture?
3. How difficult was it to put on another culture?
4. How did your own individual and cultural traits prevent you from fully adopting the East or West culture?
5. How did you plan your approach to the negotiations?
6. Did you attempt to determine how the other side might behave?
7. Were your assumptions correct?

8. Did you notice any differences in nonverbal behavior between the two groups? The use of verbal language?
9. During the negotiations, when did you first notice that there might be a problem?
10. What barriers caused this problem?
11. Was this barrier broken and productive negotiations allowed to continue?
12. What strategies were used to be culturally sensitive?
13. What strategies were used to get the artifact or keep it from the other team?
14. How could the negotiations have been more successful?

Exercise 8.2: The East-West Game

Instructions for the East

Your group represents an ancient Eastern culture that although poor, is very proud of its long history and heritage. You have a highly treasured artifact that is as old as 400 AD It is *the* national treasure and culturally you cannot give it up. The West wants this artifact and has been strongly pressured to return with it. (You may wish to identify a single behavior demonstrated by the West that will win them the artifact.)

What complicates these negotiations is that you come from a culture that is very agreeable, polite, and always seeking to answer in the affirmative whether you mean "yes" or not. You never state anything as flatly negative during negotiation sessions. You never tell your opposing team that they will never get the artifact. Sometimes you may stop the negotiations to talk amongst yourselves. You always seem to agree and go along with the other team because offending another party might result in the other losing face.

You do not use strong, direct eye contact. You occasionally look them in the eye but never for prolonged periods of time nor with any degree of intensity. Using mediation is common in your culture. For example, although the Chief Spokesman may do a lot of the talking he will very often ask his team members what they think. He will often allow other members to speak and carry on the negotiations with the other side.

Before meeting the other team, look at the following list of roles and cultural traits. Decide who will have each role, adopt the cultural traits that govern your culture, and choose an approach you will take in the negotiations.

Roles

Chief Spokesman, Minister of Education and Culture, Security Officer, Political Officer, Protocol Officer, Information Officer, Recorder (to list all the assumptions, values, etc., of other side), Time-keeper (to keep each phase exactly on schedule), GOD (Group Organizational Director) -the overall organizer of the East Team, Most Honored Grandmother, Spokesman (most honored), Advisors --- all others.

Cultural Traits

"We": The group is most highly valued, not the individual. Individual always in social role. Cannot do anything to conflict with group.
Form Outward form is most important. Manners extremely important, must participate in activities considered important by group, even if one disagrees.
Nature: Conformity to the rules of nature is best.

(Continued)

Progress: Change is both negative and positive. Technical change necessary, social change bad.

Efficiency: Considered less important than higher values such as form, saving face, conformity to custom.

Time: Not precisely measured, not primary consideration. Present, not future, given priority,

Humility: Related to one's social status. One never takes advantage of one's rank. One must always defer to one of higher social rank, must always try to appear humble.

Money: Saving for the sake of saving is seldom considered a virtue. Price is regarded as an index of quality.

Age: Great reverence for age. Age means wisdom and certain privileges. Honorific titles are always used when addressing an elder. Person of higher rank must attempt to defer to and honor special inferiors.

Education: Highly valued. Means of raising whole family status.

Authority: Obedience to authority, individual rights mean little.

Moral Superiority. A moral smugness that stems from a conviction that East people are a special people with a set of values and conditions that make them unique.

Exercise 8.2: The East-West Game

Instructions for the West

Your group represents a Western culture that is rich and powerful. There is a highly treasured artifact in the possession of the East that is a highly valued part of their heritage. They are a poor country but will be very reluctant to give up the artifact. Your national museum and your government have strongly urged you to get the artifact at any cost. Money is no problem. You cannot come out and say that you will get the artifact at any cost because the East is world renowned as shrewd traders. But you believe that every person has his/her price.

Culturally, you feel it is important to try to figure out the strategies acceptable to the other side so that you can enter and progress through the negotiations smoothly. But you should always try to stay within the cultural traits listed below. You are success-oriented, hard-working, efficient, future-oriented, and you use time productively. You like to move things along.

Before meeting the other team, look at the following list of roles and cultural traits. Decide who will have each role, adopt the cultural traits that govern your culture. and choose an approach you will take in the negotiations.

Roles

Curator of National Museum (expert on Oriental art); Millionaire (major donator of museum); Diplomatic Officer; Public Relations man or woman; CIA Agent posing as an Area Studies Specialist; Journalist; Chief of your Task-Group (forceful administrator); Recorder (to list all assumptions, values, etc., of other side); Time-keeper (to keep each phase of exercise exactly on schedule); GOD (Group Organizational Director) -- the overall organizer of the West team; Advisors -- all others

Cultural Traits

"I": Egocentric.
Individualism: Self-reliance and initiative expected from other side. Status achieved from own efforts. Achievement is good and requires competitiveness. Competition is expected.
Social Conformity: Outward conformity to opinions of others has certain value.
Activism: Being active and "on top of things," especially when uncertain, is a virtue. Achievement and goal-oriented activities stressed.
Pragmatism: Practical ingenuity applied to social and materialistic problems.
Progress: Change in itself is good. Humans must work to control nature.
Efficiency: Social organizations and individuals must be efficient.
Time: Precisely measured and must be used productively and efficiently.
Aggressiveness: Ambition, competition, and self-assertiveness to achieve success are emphasized.

Instructions for the West

(Continued)

<u>Money:</u> An economic tool and yardstick for social status, influence, power, satisfaction.

<u>Youth:</u> Highly valued. Old people wish they were young again.

<u>Education:</u> Means to an end. Reflection on family prestige. Means to attain skill, money, status.

<u>Authority:</u> Rules/laws generally obeyed, but don't like to be ordered to obey. Authority must not infringe on individual rights.

<u>Moral Superiority:</u> A moral smugness that stems from a conviction that Western people are a special people with a set of values and conditions that make them unique.

Exercise 8.3: Universal Ethics in Intercultural Communication. This activity takes students out of the classroom and is designed to be used in conjunction with Kale's article on peace as an ethic for intercultural communication. Kale indicates that:

> The concept of peace applies not only to relations between cultures and countries, but to the right of all people to live at peace with themselves and their surroundings. As such it is unethical to communicate with people in a way that does violence to their concept of themselves or to the dignity and worth of their human spirit.

With this notion in mind, have students examine recent media events to find two examples. First, have them find a media example in which this notion was NOT adhered to. Was minimal, moderate, or optimal peace the result? Compare and contrast the results if the situation were hypothetically reversed and Kale's concept of peace were applied. What level of peace could be anticipated? Second, have the students find a recent media event in which some or all of Kale's four principles for a universal code of ethics were applied. Identify the principles and the outcome of the situation. What level of peace was achieved? What might have been the result if these principles were not applied? Have students discuss their findings with the class.

Test Items for Chapter 8

<u>Multiple Choice</u>
1. What factor does Cleveland identify as a primary incentive for people to develop multiple personalities with plural group loyalties?
   a. This is a more mobile world as evidenced by the fact that in 1994 more people moved than ever before in world history. *
   b. Fear has caused people to become loyal to only one group.
   c. Political structures are being questioned.
   d. None of the above.

2. According to Cleveland, two major impediments to better standards of life and freedom for all are
   a. technology and the Internet.
   b. human rights and technology.
   c. culture and diversity. *
   d. diversity and human rights.

3. In the East, a concept understood through _____ is one of complete meaning and immediately experienced, apprehended, and contemplated.
   a. analysis
   b. emotion
   c. spiritualism
   d. intuition *

4. What does the term "undifferentiated" mean in terms of Eastern philosophy and consciousness?
   a. wholeness *
   b. uniqueness
   c. distinctness
   d. serenity

5. The relationship of the views of East and West can best be described as
   a. competing.
   b. antagonistic.
   c. complementary. *
   d. dualistic.

6. Western thought tends to equate logic with
   a. necessity.
   b. truth. *
   c. progress.
   d. correctness.

7. Which of the following does Johannesen NOT give as a defining characteristic of an ethical issue in communication?
   a. voluntarily choosing a communication strategy
   b. the communication strategy is based on a value judgment
   c. when two interactants are of unequal status *
   d. the chosen strategy could affect someone else

8. On what concept does Kale base his universal code of ethics?
   a. human spirit *
   b. human dignity
   c. humaneness
   d. human volition

9. The absence of conflict refers to what kind of peace?
   a. minimal *
   b. moderate
   c. optimal
   d. extreme

True/False

T   1.   According to Cleveland, the "civilization" construct will work because nobody is in charge of practices that are generally accepted.

F   2.   Traditions of separateness and discrimination are always permanent and immutable.

F	3.	In earlier times, the waves of new Americans learned to tolerate each other as individuals and then as groups.
T	4.	According to Kim, the Western view of the world is characteristically dualistic, materialistic, and lifeless.
T	5.	In the East, a virtuous person is not one who only strives for the "good" and eliminates the "bad" but one who strives for a balance between the two.
F	6.	The Western perception of time is best represented as a wheel that is continually turning.
F	7.	Explicit and clear verbalization best characterizes the Eastern way of communicating.
T	8.	The West is concerned more than the East with building greater ego strength.
F	9.	Morals are the basis for communication ethics.
T	10.	There is no such thing as a totally individual system of ethics.
F	11.	Moderate peace refers to the absence of conflict.
T	12.	U.S. and Canada may be said to maintain an optimal peace.

Essay Questions

1. Identify some of the reasons Cleveland believes the U.S. is growing toward pluralism.
2. How do Eastern and Western peoples view the relationship of nature and humans?
3. What is the differentiated aesthetic continuum?
4. How do Western and Eastern peoples traditionally conceptualize knowledge?
5. How do the East and West perceive time differently?
6. How do Eastern and Western views of relationships, groups, and the self differ?
7. How does one communicate one's feelings in Eastern and Western culture.
8. Describe how our lives demand both scientific and aesthetic modes of apprehension.
9. What are the benefits of incorporating an Eastern aesthetic orientation into Western life?
10. What is "intercultural personhood" and how and why should we strive to attain it?
11. What is the basic premise of cultural relativity?
12. Describe Kale's notion of the human spirit as an organizing concept on which to base a universal code of ethics.
13. Describe the three different kinds of peace mentioned by Kale.
14. On what four principles does Kale base his code of universal ethics?